Significant Choices

We make choices every day about how we shall live, and in hard times these choices can be more complicated. In our challenges, may we always seek Jesus.

A British radio programme called *Desert Island Discs* features interviews with famous people. They select favourite tracks of music, which are interspersed with the telling of their life stories. Each person is asked at the end of the programme to imagine being cast away alone on a desert island. They have the Bible and the works of Shakespeare, and can choose one other book, and one *luxury* item (nothing practical is allowed - like a box of matches!). Each person is also asked: which single piece of music would you save from the waves? Faced with such choices, I sometimes wonder what underlying priorities I would reveal in this situation.

Our readings from 1 Kings illustrate the significant choices made by the leaders of Israel and Judah. Even during the reign of David, division over power arises between and within the twelve tribes, which later become two separate kingdoms. Everybody wants to be king, but nobody seems able to fulfil the king's calling: the faithful covenant with God. We read repeatedly of the lure of idols – sometimes these are other gods; often, more simply, the desire for power.

People talk easily of 'speaking truth to power' but this is much harder to do than to say! Even Elijah the prophet struggles with his calling to speak truth – he is sometimes fearful or depressed. We must all choose our battles, because we cannot fight them all; but there are things on which we should never compromise. Some of the kings were pretty good, but mostly they hedged their bets: they did not take down the high places and commit themselves fully to God. There are high places jostling for our own attention. Let us rather dedicate ourselves each day to Jesus and hear God's call to us through his Word.

Sally Nelson
Editor

Annabel Moule
Content Assistant

ON THE COVER: **'It is God's guidance and power that move the mission forward, not human planning or strategy.'**

Image credit: Shutterstock / MarcelClemens

The Writers

DAVID SMITH is engaged in international ministry in Asia and Africa. His most recent book, *Stumbling toward Zion* highlights the importance of the biblical tradition of lament.

ANDY BATHGATE retired as CEO of SU Scotland in March 2020 after 18 years in the role. He is married to Alyson and lives in Edinburgh, where they are both involved in local church leadership.

PHILIP CHURCH is a Senior Research Fellow at Laidlaw College, Auckland, where he previously taught Biblical Studies. He remains involved in research supervision, and in teaching in the Majority World. He is a board member of A Rocha Aotearoa NZ.

STEVE WALTON is an Associate Research Fellow at Trinity College, Bristol, and serves as Secretary of the British New Testament Society. He is currently writing a commentary on Acts for the Word Biblical Commentary.

EMLYN & 'TRICIA WILLIAMS worked for Scripture Union for many years in a variety of roles, in the UK and overseas. They are now part-time editors of *Daily Bread*.

CAROLINE FLETCHER is a freelance writer based in Chesterfield who also works in media sales. She has an MPhil in Biblical Studies and has recently been working on a book about lesser-known New Testament characters.

JULIE WOODS is a freelance Old Testament lecturer who concentrates on the Majority World, though recently working more in the UK. She is currently working at London School of Theology.

SALLY NELSON is the Dean of Baptist Formation at St Hild College, Yorkshire, UK, where she also teaches Christian doctrine and pastoral care. She is a Baptist minister and has been the commissioning editor for *Encounter with God* since 2015.

ANNABEL MOULE is the content manager for *Encounter with God*. She studied English Literature at Oxford Brookes University and Theology at the University of Oxford.

Contents

Scripture Union is a member of the worldwide Scripture Union international community.
Website: https://scriptureunion.global

THE GOD OF SURPRISES

In under a year, Fiona Beck has become both a children's and families' worker and a Faith Guide, and has established an incredibly popular after-school club. She has set her sights and prayers on it becoming a Grow Community and the first green shoots of faith are already appearing.

Fiona has a long history with Scripture Union; she became a Christian on an SU camp in Scotland, became a leader at 17 and later started volunteering regularly at Port St Mary Beach Mission, which is where she met her husband. Sarah Howard-Smith, SU North Support Worker, visited the Beach Mission in the summer of 2021 and shared the Revealing Jesus mission framework and talked about being a Faith Guide. 'I thought it was a great idea,' Fiona says, 'but at the time I felt it wasn't for me.'

'God of course knew different! Before I went home, a godly couple prayed with me and I felt led to look at a Christian jobs website and saw that St Andrew's Church in Cheadle Hulme (near my home) was looking for a children's worker. I'd been working in a supermarket, although it was my volunteering with church and with SU that defined me. So I applied for the church role and, to my amazement, I got the job. I never saw that coming! Now I had every reason to be a Faith Guide, so I signed up, did my training and began planning what to do next.'

Wonderful church support

Over a number of years, the church had lost the few families it had, so they were very keen to reach out to children and young people in the wider community. They were so keen, in fact, that 35 of the 50 congregation members volunteered to help Fiona. 'I only work 20 hours a week,' Fiona says, 'so I have felt really blessed by their support. I try to align the roles with what they like doing and are good at. So far it's worked!'

> '... I had every reason to be a Faith Guide, so I signed up, did my training and began planning what to do next.'

Making connections with families

SU's Revealing Jesus mission framework incorporates four stages: Connect, Explore, Respond and Grow. Within weeks of starting in her new role in September, Fiona and her team of volunteers began to connect with local children and their families. 'We organised a Light Party using SU materials to create a Light Trail,' says Fiona. 'In the best tradition, it poured

mums-and-tots groups which has around seventy members in all. We also put on other events, connected with local schools and promoted K@STA on Facebook. We prayed and left it in God's hands.'

'God's been so good to us'

Fiona was astonished when 29 children arrived for the first K@STA session! She says, 'Word must have gone around the playground because the next week 51 turned up and soon we had to start a waiting list. By the time we broke up for summer, over a hundred and thirty children, mostly from non-Christian homes, had attended the club since it began seven months earlier. Not all come to every session – the average weekly attendance is around fifty. God's been so good to us, we've never had an unmanageable number.'

with rain, everyone got wet and we all had to come inside! But we got chatting to parents over refreshments and it started to get me known in the community.'

Fiona was already looking ahead to the next stages of the faith journey with plans to launch an after-school club, K@STA (Kasta, or Kids@St Andrews), in the January. 'Meantime, we continued to build up connections with children and families,' she says. 'I took on the running of the

'It's amazing to think that the number of children at the club each week matches the number of people in the entire church congregation!'

Friday night fun

K@STA takes place on a Friday night. Fiona says, 'We have three groups in different rooms. For the first half hour it's free time and they can do whatever activities they fancy. We have football, or another organised game, for the active ones, board games in another room and a quieter craft room where children can just hang out and chat. That's something we introduced in response to a request from some of the older girls. We were so busy keeping them busy that they said there wasn't enough time to sit and ask the leaders questions about things that were on their minds!

'Then we go through to the church. We sing a couple of songs, with an activity in between. For the first half term we had "twenty questions" with the leaders. There were some fun questions involved, to help engage the quieter children, but also more serious questions around why they believe in God. The next half term, we used some short animation videos where Jesus comes on and talks about a particular theme from the gospels. Then the final term we evolved the teaching once more and started asking three questions about the video for them to discuss with a leader in small friendship groups. Towards the end of the summer term, we opted to go back to free play again after refreshments, hoping that some of the children would engage with the leaders about the Bible Story they had just heard.'

Journeys towards faith

One local mum has seven children. Fiona says, 'She brought her youngest to the mums-and-tots group. I got chatting with her and it turned out that she had six other children. I told her about K@STA and she said that she was sure they would love to come to the club. But she was worried too as one child is thought to have autism. We talked it through and I said, "Well, let's have a go and see how it works out" and actually it's been great.'

When Fiona and SU Mission Enabler Sarah Davison ran a Diary of a Disciple Holiday Club at Easter, those children came to that as well. Then the oldest three went to SU's Edale Holiday with Fiona. 'Initially they bickered,' she recalls, 'but we really began to see a positive change in their behaviour. Their mum has started putting prayer requests into our prayer box at church, so I hope she is on the journey towards faith too!'

Perhaps the most exciting development is one five-year-old saying to her mum that she wanted to become a Christian after just a few weeks at K@STA.

'Her mum came to me and said, "What does that even mean, being a Christian?" So I told her more about what we believe and prayed with her daughter, who now wants to be baptised. I can't say I saw that coming, either!'

'During this adventure, God has shown that he is truly full of delightful surprises. I wonder what the next one will be!'

A shorter version of this story first appeared in *Connecting You*, Scripture Union's free quarterly supporter magazine. If you'd like to receive copies of *Connecting You* and learn more of how God is moving in the hearts and lives of children and young people today, you can sign up online at su.org.uk/connectingyou.

Using this Guide

Encounter with God is designed for thinking Christians who want to interpret and apply the Bible in a way that is relevant to the problems and issues of today's world. It is based on the NIV translation of the Bible, but can easily be used with any other version.

Each set of readings begins with an *Introduction* to the section you are about to study. The *Call to Worship* section at the start of each note should help you consciously to come into God's presence before you read the passage. The main *Explore* section aims to bring out the riches hidden in the text. The *Growing in Faith* section at the end suggests ways of applying the message to daily living.

The *Bible in a Year* readings at the foot of the page are for those who want this additional option.

FROM JERUSALEM TO THE ENDS OF THE EARTH

Over the next few weeks we have the privilege of reflecting together on the marvellous story of the creation and growth of the movement which Luke identifies as followers of 'the Way'.[1] The narrative of the book of Acts is carefully structured to describe the expansion of this movement from its origins in Palestine, specifically in Jerusalem, across the Mediterranean world and reaching its climax in the imperial capital – the city of Rome. In the course of this story, Acts charts the first great cross-cultural spread of what came to be called 'Christianity'. In contrast to the modern missionary movement, this one began at the margins of the empire and was carried to the centre by people, many of whom were migrants or slaves, who had discovered in Jesus of Nazareth the Saviour of the whole inhabited world.

It is very important to notice the connection between this story and that contained in Luke's Gospel, which the author here describes as 'my former book' (1:1). I suggest pausing here to read Luke 1:1–4, where Luke explains the purpose of all of his work. Notice that in both volumes he addresses 'Theophilus', whom he describes as 'most excellent'[2] – suggesting a person of high status and honour who is curious concerning the people of the Way.

Luke himself was well educated and had a privileged background, and he narrates the story of Jesus and his followers in response to growing numbers of Gentile enquirers who are attracted to the Jesus movement. In other words, Luke writes to privileged people who are fascinated by the spread of a community which embodied the radical teaching of Jesus of Nazareth. The story told in Acts makes very clear the personal, economic and relational costs of following Jesus.[3] Be prepared for the book of Acts to present serious challenges concerning the life of discipleship today!

David Smith

---

[1] Eg Acts 24:14 [2] Luke 1:3 [3] See Karl Allen Kuhn, *Luke The Elite Evangelist*, Liturgical Press, 2010

Acts 12:19b–24

The Word That Endures

Enable us, Lord, to recognise the challenge of this strange text to our broken world.

The contrast between the description of Herod at the end of our previous reading, callously ordering the execution of sixteen guards as though their lives counted for nothing, and this account of his sudden and humiliating death is very striking. The incident in Caesarea highlights both the terrible social and economic consequences of tyranny and oppression, and the insane hubris of rulers who exercise absolute power and believe their own propaganda.

In the dispute between Herod and the people of Tyre and Sidon, the issue seems to have been economic – specifically the region's food supply. Luke implies that the Herodian system had created a structure of dependency, in which these people were driven to pleading with their ruler for the basic necessities of life. They had found an intermediary, Blastus, who secured them an audience. The description shows the dominating nature of absolute power and the humiliation and subservience it inflicts upon poor and hungry people. Not only so, but when Herod deigns to appear in person, the crowd responds with cries of adulation and a display of loyalty which they know to be the precondition for their very survival.

We should not read this story as though it concerns ancient history and is remote from our realities in the twenty-first century. Millions of people across the world today suffer deprivation and hunger, finding themselves locked into economic systems that condemn them to dependency and the need to beg for aid and support. That being so, the nature of Herod's demise should give us pause for thought! Unjust political systems, whether led by tyrannical individuals or justified by elaborate ideological theories, are contrary to the will of God and counter to his Word, which 'continued to spread and flourish' (v 24). The daily reading of the Bible remains a potentially subversive activity!

Give thanks that the Word of God continues to 'spread and flourish'.

BIBLE IN A YEAR: **2 Chronicles 33,34; Psalms 75,76**

Holy is the Lord

Enable us, Lord, to measure our public worship against the standard set in this psalm.

The dominant theme of this little hymn is the holiness of God (vs 3,5,9). Everything in it serves to illustrate and emphasise this characteristic of Israel's God. Although the divine nature has been revealed to Israel specifically – Moses, Aaron and Samuel are singled out as bearers of the revelation of his character – it is also available for 'all the nations' (vs 2,3) and they are summoned to join the song of praise and adoration.

The second stanza (vs 4,5) connects the core divine attribute of holiness with justice, equity and what is right, pointing to the fact that God's nature has practical and societal consequences and that to worship him in truth must result in a way of life which mirrors his character. This is, of course, the constant theme of Israel's prophets, who demanded that splendid public worship in the Temple must have social consequences in 'what is just and right' (v 4). Bereft of this, it degenerates into an empty and powerless ritual. The knowledge of God is traced to a theophany in which he spoke to the fathers 'from the pillar of cloud', which resulted in their keeping 'his statutes and the decrees he gave them' (v 7).

Finally, the holiness of God and the demand this makes upon his worshippers for 'what is just and right' (v 4), means that human beings will inevitably be conscious of sin and failure; for this reason the psalmist rejoices that 'you were to Israel a forgiving God, though you punished their misdeeds' (v 8). Weiser comments that awe and terror are combined in this hymn with joyful confidence and he says that it is the combination of these two experiences which alone 'produce the true note of biblical faith'.[1] We should ask ourselves how our public worship measures up against this standard.

Reread the psalm, then pray the Lord's Prayer and note the parallels.

[1] Artur Weiser, *The Psalms: A Commentary*, Westminster Press, 1962

BIBLE IN A YEAR: **2 Chronicles 35,36; Luke 1:39–80**

Isaiah 1-21

VISIONS OF JUDGEMENT AND HOPE

Isaiah 1–21 involves us in 'unremittingly dark' passages of judgement (chs 1,3–5; 9:8 – 10:34; 13; 15–21) and 'unbelievably bright'[1] messages of hope (chs 2; 9:1–7; 11,12,14). The transitions are stark, leaving us somewhat disorientated. These ups and downs help us to interpret our world, providing a warning not to become overly pessimistic or triumphalist about the future. We are called to examine the extent of our sin and to rejoice in the purposes of God.

Isaiah conducts a probing examination and condemnation of sin, lack of concern for the poor and disadvantaged being a prime target. Prophecies are mainly directed at the southern kingdom of Judah, although later chapters speak against the nations surrounding Judah, including Israel: chapters 13–21 speak to northern powers (chs 13,14,21), near neighbours (chs 14–17) and southern powers (chs 18–20). The fierce expressions of disaster to come should be read in the context of two factors. First, the disciplinary chastisements are aimed at alerting God's people to their deviations from his character and calling them back to himself. Second, and relatedly, they are often conditional. As in Jonah, a repentant heart brings release from the consequences of rebellion. Sadly, the warnings largely go unheeded, which means disaster for Judah, but not obliteration. In God's mercy, a remnant will remain. He will restore and begin his work with these few. Small children become signs of God's promised kingdom (chs 7–11).

The setting for these visions is seldom made explicit. That is partly explained by their relevance to many contexts and generations. Tying them too tightly to historical circumstances may lessen their applicability. However, Isaiah does set out his historical context in chapters 1 and 6, pointing to a period around 740–700 BC, ending with the threat of Assyrian attack on Jerusalem. The Assyrians are the major threat of these chapters. The test for Judah (and also for us) is where they will look for help in addressing their fears – to God or to others?

Andy Bathgate

---

[1] John N Oswalt, *The Holy One of Israel*, Cascade, 2014, p4

Family Unlikeness

'In you all can be found. Why should I look elsewhere or go elsewhere? You have the words of eternal life, you are the Way, the Truth, and the Life.'[1]

It's not always clear why settled, loving homes sometimes produce rebellious children. In Philip Roth's novel, *American Pastoral*,[2] the daughter of a devoted and morally assiduous father is exposed as a terrorist. This mirrors the Lord's experience. His covenant love, which nurtures his children, is 'rebelled against' (v 2) and 'spurned' (v 4), leaving him 'forsaken' (v 4). Turning their backs on God, the people behave like strangers to their family, the images of disloyalty comparing unfavourably with farm animals who understand their dependence on their owners (v 3). The New Testament warns *us* not to forsake our first love.[3]

The Holy One of Israel (v 4) cannot simply ignore or indulge their ingratitude. It provokes a 'woe' on his own children and disciplinary action to alert them to the profound consequences of their folly. Sinful behaviour has dire consequences for the health of a nation and its environment (v 7). Judah is in ruins, as enemies, strangers and foreign nations gain the ascendency. Judah, however, is still considered a daughter (v 8). That cannot change.

But, the people of Judah are never entirely abandoned. Their plight would be like that of the totally destroyed Sodom and Gomorrah unless the Lord had other plans (v 9). They will avoid destruction, but not by the means they think. The remedy does not lie in trying to appease God with outward signs of devotion, which will multiply his anger or simply bore him (vs 14,15). What does God look for? Refraining from doing wrong and starting to care for the oppressed, the orphans and the widows, grasping what he is concerned for. Their repentance must be about loving their neighbours as they love themselves.

Can our worship sometimes distract us from what God really wants from us? Talk about how to be alert to ritual that is divorced from genuine penitence and transformed attitudes.

---

[1] From a prayer by Henri Nouwen [2] Philip Roth, *American Pastoral*, Vintage, 1998 [3] Rev 2:4

BIBLE IN A YEAR: **Ezra 1,2; Luke 2**

Spiritual Abuse

Meditate on the descriptions of God in verse 24 and turn your thoughts into a prayer of reverent worship and thanks.

Massive decline can be traced in Jerusalem's history. The once great city has lost its status as a place recognised for its loyalty to God. Its lofty standards of justice and righteousness have vanished. The litmus test is defence of the vulnerable (v 23). This is the second time that Isaiah has focused on orphans and widows (see also v 17). They receive a prominence that is too often overlooked. The powerful in Jerusalem are more interested in lining their pockets than supporting the needy. That's not unusual. The abuse of power repeatedly sees leaders accumulate wealth while thousands starve or disappear. Mobutu's international airport and colossal mansion built in his home village, where there was no running water or electricity, is but one example.[1] Jerusalem is worse. This is God's people oppressing their own, behaving like heathen idol-worshippers. Scarily, it turns them into enemies (vs 24,25) of the Lord, the Mighty One.

Peter warns that God's judgement begins with God's household.[2] Far from being exempt, God's people come under scrutiny as those who should know how to live, making just decisions and modelling right behaviour. What is his purpose in turning his hand against his people? It is redemptive intervention with the aim of purification and restoration (vs 25,26).

Such is God's restoring power that there will again be a city called 'righteous' and 'faithful'. This is the kind of transformation that will create a new heaven and new earth. There will be deliverance, but that inevitably means punishment and shame for some (vs 28,29). Oaks with fading leaves and unwatered gardens present a picture of the fruitlessness of those who disown the Lord, much as of those who do not remain in Christ and are ineffectual.

Give thanks for your security in Christ's love. Then spend time reflecting on the link between remaining in Christ's love and your church's concern for the disadvantaged.

[1] Mobutu Sese Seko, President of Congo/Zaïre, 1930–97 [2] 1 Pet 4:17

BIBLE IN A YEAR: **Ezra 3,4; Luke 3**

Tourist Attraction?

'The word that shines from Zion's hill / shall lighten every land. / Our Saviour King shall teach his ways / and countless hearts command.'[1]

What is God's vision? Here is a remarkable picture of what God aims to do 'In the last days' (v 2; no timescale is specified). Now fire[2] is replaced by blessing. God establishes a rule which demonstrates his superiority. His Temple, located on the highest mountain, is not overlooked or dominated by anything (v 2). This mountain-top Temple is not only a sign of greatness; there is also a teaching function. People stream to this place of pilgrimage, not as a site of historical interest or must-see location on a tourist trail, but as a place of teaching and learning: a place to learn how to live well. The Lord is the attraction, his ability to judge right being the major draw (v 4).

The whole scene is one of peace. This is God's vision, and it will come about as his people (v 5) walk in the light of the Lord. Surveys tell us that the attractiveness of believers is a primary means of drawing people to God.

That is the future; what about now? The vision comes to an abrupt and jarring note in verse 6. The people who should be teaching the nations truth and sharing God's peace are abandoned by God. Their lives are 'full', but with all the wrong things – superstitions (v 6), silver and gold (v 7), horses and chariots (v 7– effectively weapon systems!) and idols (v 8). Outward prosperity betrays inner emptiness. You can gain the entire world and still be a loser if you trust something or someone other than God (v 22). A work of humbling is necessary (vs 9–21). We live in a similar tension in a church that is the beautiful bride of Christ yet too often displays the ugliness of abusive power and a reliance on our ingenuity and resourcefulness.

God will deal with his people to bring about his vision. How can we display that fruit of humility that God so clearly cherishes?

[1] Michael Bruce, 1746–67, 'Behold the Mountain of the Lord', adapted [2] Isa 1:31

BIBLE IN A YEAR: **Ezra 5,6; Psalm 77**

Isaiah 3:1 – 4:1

Chaos Reigns

Lord Almighty, search my heart and enable me to set aside everything that acts as a distraction from you. Please lead me away from trivialities and into your path.

The writer Aleksandr Solzhenitsyn recounted the time when 'a number of older people offer[ed] the following explanation for the great disasters that had befallen Russia: "Men have forgotten God"'.[1] When a society abandons God for idols and trusts human intellect, wisdom and power, chaos ensues. Isaiah dissects the outcomes for Israel when God withdraws his support, much as the apostle Paul analyses the impact of a world in which God removes his restraint.[2] We have already heard the damning word 'abandoned'.[3] Now we see its full implications, particularly in regard to leadership. It is said that people get the leadership they deserve. In this case there is a leadership vacuum (vs 4,6,7), with no one willing to take on responsibility. Without leaders, oppression is rife (and, as always, it's the poor who suffer; v 15) and there is a disruption of relationships and values (vs 5,12). Without a moral compass, sin is no longer a cause for shame (v 9). Everything is in turmoil.

Does this seem extreme? It certainly pinpoints the logical conclusion of rejecting all that is gained from a Christian heritage. Function as if there is no God, and see what it brings. This should bring us to our knees in repentance, though we give thanks that the Holy Spirit is at work to convict the world about sin, righteousness and judgement.[4] There is, as always, a word of hope (v 10), but it is tucked in among many causes for grief. These continue as Isaiah catalogues self-indulgent obsessions with sex, fashion and image (vs 16–23), all very prominent contemporary preoccupations. God wants to bring his people to lament (v 26) by demonstrating how pointless life becomes without him to lead us.

We are all leaders somewhere: pray that God's Spirit will guide as you exercise your leadership.

[1] Aleksandr Solzhenitsyn, Templeton Address, 1983 [2] Rom 1:24–32 [3] Isa 2:6 [4] John 16:8–11

BIBLE IN A YEAR: **Ezra 7,8; Luke 4**

Beauty from Ashes

Teach me, Lord, to trust in you, even in the calamities of this life. Help me to know that catastrophe is never the last word where you are present.

We continue the roller-coaster ride of these early chapters of Isaiah. After the depths of the previous chapters ('woe', 'abandoned', 'judgement'), we are now ratcheted up into the heights, with views of breathtaking beauty. God's 'strange' work of judgement[1] includes the creation of something 'beautiful and glorious' (v 2) following the purging of evil.

John Oswalt explains, 'The Israelites and Judeans thought, as many moderns do, that judgement and hope are contrasting elements. But Isaiah shows that they are complementary … there is hope, but it is through judgement'.[2] Even severe judgement leaves survivors (vs 2,3, literally 'people who escaped'). The implication is that they are few, but they will be called 'holy' with their names written in God's book (v 3). Deluge and fire will wash clean and burn away impurity (v 4). God often prunes in order to promote growth,

making the results of his work at times seem small and vulnerable. Terrifying judgement and reduction to a remnant could be a disastrous strategy if it were not for God's overarching protection, creating a refuge for his people (vs 5,6). He is, after all, the God of the Exodus, still present to lead, guide and safeguard. Without that promise, we would never persevere.

The Greek Island of Evia suffered devastating fires in the summer of 2020. Visits there show entire hillsides of blackened, burnt-out trees and vegetation, a lunar landscape where livelihoods have been ruined. However, in 2022 masses of wild flowers in vibrant reds, yellows and purples brighten and beautify the otherwise-dead landscape. There is life, not just existence, but extravagance of colour, brightness and beauty. Just as God spoke and brought creation out of chaos, so he will speak again.

Have you lost hope of change in some area of life? Does this passage shed any light on it? Perhaps only a flicker, reminding you that God is at work.

[1] Isa 28:21 [2] John N Oswalt, *The Holy One of Israel*, Cascade, 2014, p19

BIBLE IN A YEAR: **Ezra 9,10; Luke 5**

Fruitless Endeavour

Give thanks for ways in which God has blessed and nurtured you in your life. Name those who have been God's means of discipling you.

Isaiah the folk singer starts up a love song which quickly takes on a blues feel. He moves from Cliff Richard to Leonard Cohen and remains in that darker mood without the respite that we have come to expect in his passages of hope. He sings on behalf of a vineyard owner. The effort put into nurturing the vineyard or relationship is unstinting and carries expectations (notice the repeated 'looked' in verses 2, 4 and 7). The building of a watchtower and the construction of a winepress indicate that there is a crop needing to be protected and developed.

Our minds turn to Jesus' assertion, 'I am the true vine'.[1] He, too, expects fruit with increasing yields in response to the love he showers on us. Fruit is no optional extra but a necessary consequence of being in Jesus. Here there is nothing to show for all the sustained nurture. The relationship lacks any mutuality. The result? The vineyard is turned back into wasteland. Delight (v 7) turns to disappointment and soon we shall see what this will mean for Jerusalem (vs 26–30).

What was this expected fruit? Justice and righteousness (v 7), interpreted later by Jesus as sacrificial love for others.[2] This is about treatment of other people. Bloodshed and cries of distress are the marks of a fruitless people. This could involve actual murders but may equally refer to policies in the nation that effectively killed the vulnerable. Much of the teaching in the New Testament epistles is devoted to how we relate to one another. James, for example, warns against quarrels that are tantamount to murder.[3] This is abhorrent to the Lord to the point where he tears things down, allowing a slide into disarray. It is an enormously chilling prospect – God withdrawing from his people.

Start positively by giving thanks for all the expressions of fruitfulness you see in your community of faith. Then also consider where justice and righteousness may be absent.

[1] John 15:1 [2] John 15:12 [3] James 4:1–3

BIBLE IN A YEAR: **Nehemiah 1,2; Psalm 78:1–37**

Shout and Sing!

'Joy to the world! The Lord is come.'[1] We receive you, we acknowledge your goodness and we give you thanks that your coming sets us free for joy.

We live in a messy and often painful world. Personally and communally we face the trauma of loss, the disappointment of unfaithfulness, the senselessness of violence, the unfairness of injustice. They cause us deep anxiety, frustration and despondency. The psalms do not ignore this aspect of life: they provide us with words to express our troubled mindset. However, they also recognise that lamenting and soul-searching need to be counterbalanced by a heart of joy. Not a manufactured, forced joy, but one that arises from reflecting on the gratitude we owe to God. Psalm 100 calls us to a joyful response, without hesitation or reluctance.

There are reasons to shout and sing, to be glad and thankful. Everyone ('all the earth', v 1) can and should join the chorus. No one should be left out of this joyous celebration. After all, the darker side of life does not mean we are victims of fate and inexplicable forces. There is a God and he is the covenant-making Lord who creates people and makes them his own. Our universe is not some impersonal place, meaningless and random, with us as insignificant bags of molecules that have a brief and lonely stay. The God who made it also tends it, like a good shepherd caring for each of his flock. We derive our identity and value from the one who has proved to be 'good' (v 5), one who has patiently stuck with us in faithful love. Even the rough times are interpreted through this lens of goodness, knowing that there is a bigger purpose at work. Jesus expressed his desire that we know his joy and that our joy may be complete.[2] That joy starts with the words, 'I have loved you'.[3]

What truly brings you joy? Give thanks to God as the giver of every good gift, for the joy he brings. How can you share this joy with others?

[1] Isaac Watts, 1674–1748 [2] John 15:11 [3] See John 15:9

BIBLE IN A YEAR: **Nehemiah 3,4; Luke 6**

Isaiah 5:8–30

Pleasure Palaces

Teach me, Lord, that you alone are the one who 'satisfies the thirsty and fills the hungry with good things'.[1]

Rampant consumerism, hedonism, disregard for God, being convinced of our intellectual superiority and making decisions based on our own whims. You may think that's a description of contemporary society. In fact, it's an exposé of Judah (vs 8–24) which results in a complaint (v 7). The Lord sees lack of justice and righteousness. He sees oppression of people whose cries for help are ignored. These verses contain six 'woe's that Isaiah utters against the people:[2] 'woe's that are as much a cry of pain for abysmal behaviour as they are expressions of condemnation.[3] Justice fails and righteousness fades when self-indulgence rules.

Self-indulgence can quickly cut us off from the cries of others. Isaiah describes mansions in their own grounds, gated communities without any connection to their local community. They will end up like so many derelict stately homes in the UK. There will be large outlays with minimal return (v 10). Pleasure-seeking also inures us to the needs of others. Wild parties give little time for regarding the deeds of the Lord or 'the work of his hands' (v 12), which must include people made in his image. Only sharing the plight of the displaced in exile (v 13) or death itself (v 14) will be enough to shake these people. Humbling becomes a priority when people mock God's judgement (v 19). All this will serve to prove God's holiness, meaning not just his exalted status but also his righteousness. His purpose will prevail and as the Mighty God he can even draw on heathen nations to accomplish it (v 26). These nations will act unknowingly on his behalf, to prune his recalcitrant people. Isaiah's first section thus ends in despair.

We must be careful not to allow this passage to become a basis for taking the moral high ground and criticising society. It must lead to self-reflection and tears.

[1] Ps 107:9 [2] With a seventh 'woe' in Isa 10:1-4 [3] John Goldingay, *Isaiah – Understanding the Bible*, Baker Books, 2001

BIBLE IN A YEAR: **Nehemiah 5,6; Luke 7**

Overwhelming Encounter

'O Jesus Christ, grow thou in me, / and all things else recede; ... That I am nothing, thou art all, / I would be daily taught.'[1]

Chapter 5 ended with a threat: an imminent Assyrian attack (and future Babylonian invasion?). Chapter 6 begins with a death – hardly a promising start. It marks a significant transition, since King Uzziah had overseen great prosperity in his 52-year reign. The king is dead, long live *The* King, he who surpasses all other monarchs. He has no limitations in his might (all-mighty), his holiness (three times over, in verse 3) or the scope of his reign (the whole earth). The magnificent Temple cannot contain him. Encountering his holiness means confronting our frailty and sinfulness. Isaiah is 'undone' and 'dismantled'.[2] He stands as a representative of a defiled nation, incapable of being the Lord's servant. We have to examine any behaviour that denies our God: 'I hold this against you' is the word to Revelation's churches.[3]

We are incapable of being God's true representatives and speaking his truth. The solution? God's initiative in cleansing (v 7). Such holiness is frightening, revealing our distance from God's perfection, but 'Merciful grace belongs as much to the essence of holiness as justice and purity'.[4] Isaiah is restored to the unenviable task of speaking God's truth. It will be a word of judgement and hardening; a protracted process of refining and pruning, before a stump remains to issue a shoot in the future (v 13).[5]

Israel was meant to be a witness to truth and justice, reflecting the character of a holy God, but it knows neither the greatness of God nor its own uncleanness. The people could not be witnesses until they acknowledged both. Isaiah gets it and volunteers for the somewhat thankless task which will confirm some in their rebellion. It will be a long and painful road, but life will never be extinguished. God will not quench the flame, however low it flickers.

Could you gather with others to·seek God and to acknowledge your part in society's ills?

---

[1] Johann Casper Lavater, 1741–1801 [2] Walter Brueggemann, *Isaiah 1–39*, Westminster, 1998, p59 [3] Rev 2:4,14,20 [4] John Goldingay, *Isaiah*, 2001 [5] Isa 11:1; 37:31

BIBLE IN A YEAR: **Nehemiah 7,8; Luke 8**

Isaiah 7

No Faith, no Future

'A mighty fortress is our God, / a bulwark never failing'.[1] Express your renewed trust in this God.

Who will you trust when things get sticky? When everything is going right, the sky is clear and the sun is shining, it's a doddle to trust God! But when the pressure is on? Isaiah confronts a king threatened to the point of terror by near neighbours Aram (Syria) and Israel (or Ephraim), who in turn are menaced by Assyria. Already the king is out safeguarding the water supply in the event of a siege (v 3). 'Keep calm' and 'Don't be afraid' (see v 4) seem hollow words when everything appears against you, but God looks for trust. He is the God who created the 'house of David' (vs 2,13) with protective promises[2] and he now reiterates his Word. 'You of little faith',[3] Jesus says to his disciples when there is good reason to trust. Isaiah reveals how things will end (vs 7–9) and sets out a timescale that is also in God's hands (v 16). The sign is a baby whose name declares 'God with us' (v 14), standing by our sides whatever transpires.

Perspective changes massively when we are not consumed by fear.

Ahaz chooses on behalf of the nation, rejecting any sign from God. Thus, the greater fear of human armies overcomes trust in God. There is both warning and hope in this story. Isaiah's child's name (v 3) reveals both. Shear-Jashub, meaning 'a remnant will return', is at once a threat ('only' a remnant will be left) and a hope (God will ensure 'at least' a remnant will be left). In God's purposes, both will be true. Rejecting trust in God will lead to the four 'in that day' images of verses 18–25. They emphasise God's global power, which can call on nations to humble his people and disturb nature to produce uninhabitable land. Even in the cataclysm, however, the few who remain will be fed (v 22).

Are there decisions we make as individuals and churches which are from fear rather than faith? What can we do to change our perspective?

[1] Martin Luther, 1483–1546; tr Frederick Henry Hedge, 1805–90 [2] 2 Sam 7 [3] Matt 8:26

BIBLE IN A YEAR: **Nehemiah 9,10; Psalm 78:38–72**

A Greater Fear

Lord, I have many fears in this world. Give me grace to trust and to wait, resting in all that you are and have promised.

Another child is born, another sign is given. It's another word of warning, of judgement. Assyria is coming, having been given a role by God to overwhelm Judah's opponents, Israel and Syria (v 4). However, the brutal Assyrians won't stop there. Like a flood, they will submerge Judah too (v 8). When God's people take pleasure in the Assyrian attacks on their enemies (v 6) they disregard their own lack of immunity from judgement. The child's name, Maher-Shalal-Hash-Baz, says it clearly – judgement is coming and it's coming soon.

The call on Immanuel (meaning 'God with us', v 8) follows a judgement of unbelief as well as an assurance of protection (v 10). This same tension of hope and judgement is reflected in the stone imagery of verse 14. God as a rock is both shelter and stumbling block. Complacency and judgementalism have no part in the thinking of the people of God.

The Assyrians are one example, but all human forces are under the command of God. In their pride, they must never assume independent authority. They may make deadly plans, but they will be thwarted (v 10). So, which is the greater fear – that of being in the hands of the Assyrians or the hands of the Lord Almighty? For Isaiah there's no question – 'he is the one you are to dread' (v 13); 'I will put my trust in him' (v 17).

With enemies in the ascendancy and fear of what human power can do to us at its most fierce, where do we turn? What signs has God given *us*? In Isaiah, two children. We know that the cross and resurrection witness to human power trying to do away with the Christ of God but also to 'God with us' in salvation, in resurrection power, in the defeat of sin and death. He has overcome the world.

Isaiah is confident, but knows he has to 'wait for the LORD' (v 17). How are you getting on with waiting? Who can you encourage in a time of waiting?

BIBLE IN A YEAR: **Nehemiah 11,12; Luke 9**

Isaiah 8:19 – 9:7

To us, a Son!

'O loving wisdom of our God! / When all was sin and shame, / a second Adam to the fight / and to the rescue came.'[1]

'I am making everything new!'[2] These words could describe the transformation from the empty darkness of 8:19–22 to the vision of light of 9:1–7. Brueggemann calls it something 'completely fresh and without extrapolation from anything that has gone before'.[3] Isaiah criticises a culture that disdains the wisdom of the Lord Almighty, seeking direction from other spiritual sources and refusing to listen to God (vs 19,20). It leaves them, in Paul's words, 'darkened in their understanding and separated from the life of God'.[4] In current British culture, the phrase 'follow the science' has become common. If this means excluding the living God from discussion, something fundamental is missing from every argument, with fearful and distressing consequences (v 22).

This despair can only be overcome by the 'zeal' (9:7) or passion of God, which touches even lands that have long been in death-like darkness. Isaiah's images of harvest and military victory catch something of the elation. Drawing on Gideon's defeat of the Midianites (v 4) is particularly poignant, given the unexpected victory with a tiny force of men. Peace has come and the enemy is humiliated – and it starts small, with the birth of a child. What follows goes way beyond what any human king could aspire to. This King plans without the limited knowledge that dogs earthly kings; his might is great but not unregulated. It is under the control of Father-like love and desire for shalom, justice and righteousness. There is no end, geographically or temporally, to his reign. This cannot apply to any coming human king, even the lauded Hezekiah. Isaiah was unaware of the full future, but we recognise in this the coming of the kingdom of God, inaugurated in our Lord Jesus Christ and ending in everything being made new.

Passages like this bring us to our knees in worship, rather than to discussion. Allow these descriptions of the coming king to form prayers of deep gratitude.

[1] JH Newman, 1801–90, 'Praise to the Holiest in the height' [2] Rev 21:5 [3] Walter Brueggemann, *Isaiah 1–39*, 1998, p82 [4] Eph 4:18

BIBLE IN A YEAR: **Nehemiah 13; Luke 10**

Unending Misery?

Give me, Lord, a softness of heart, so that when you speak into my life I am ready to say, 'Your servant is listening'.[1]

Isaiah now addresses the northern tribes of Israel (Jacob / Ephraim). In a cheerless passage, did you get a jolt reading that the Lord will not 'pity the fatherless and widows' (v 17)? Surely, caring for the disadvantaged was the very thing he was known for, and his main complaint against Judah was their failure to do so.[2] Have things really gone so far downhill that the Lord has lost his compassion for those at the bottom of the pile? It seems that even they do not get a 'get out of jail free card' enabling them to escape responsibility for their actions before God. Every level of society ('both head and tail', v 14) is liable for their proud refusal to listen to the Lord. Frighteningly, after each expression of judgement we are told that 'for all this, his anger has not turned away' and his hand is 'still upraised' (vs 12,17,21). God is a completer-finisher and will continue to work in the longing that they will return to him (v 13), even when it involves a painful and grievous path involving a breakdown of family relationships (vs 19–21).

Few people perceived God's hand in their downfall. I guess we can also struggle to live in the light of his presence and purpose. We too can fall into the trap of thinking we can fix things ourselves rather than seek the mercy of God (v 10). We dither around with our schemes and strategies and forget to fall on our faces. Discerning God's discipline in our lives and responding to it is fundamental to producing a 'harvest of righteousness'.[3] Misinterpreting it has the danger of producing bitterness as opposed to repentance.[4] These people have adopted a hard-heartedness which failed to recognise God's hand.

What experience have you had of God's discipline? How did it feel? What has it produced in you? Is there someone you see veering into bitterness who needs your help?

[1] 1 Sam 3:10 [2] Isa 1:17 [3] James 3:18 [4] Heb 12, especially vs 11,15

BIBLE IN A YEAR: **Esther 1–3; Psalm 79**

A Life in Politics

'...choose for yourselves this day whom you will serve'.[1] Express your response to this choice in a prayer of dedication.

We could call this psalm 'the politician's prayer'! It is almost certainly King David's expression of his longing for integrity in his personal and political life. If he is to rule the nation well, both he and his team (his 'house', v 2) must carry themselves with honesty and trustworthiness. David has significant authority in the nation (v 8), but we should not limit this prayer to great leaders. More widely, it expresses a concern for a life that reflects the love and justice of God. That's where David starts, with God and his desire to be like him in all his interactions. If this is to happen, he needs God to 'come to me' (v 2), to convey his presence and grace. In this desire, we see the well-balanced juxtaposition of the psalms. Psalm 100 was all about uninhibited joy in God. That's no world-renouncing, self-indulgent experience. It must be lived out in the context of a 'blameless' life (v 2), even in the complicated area of national government.

Part of being 'blameless' before God is to renounce evil. David will choose carefully what he approves of and what he hates. We can never be casual about who we listen to or whose company we keep. Politics is rife with intrigue, vilification of others and self-promotion, although none of these are restricted to the political world! They are all things David will call out and refuse to tolerate. Instead, he will promote and draw on those who are faithful and servant-hearted. These are high standards. Sadly, as we look at the life of David, we know that he did not always live by them. That makes us especially grateful to one of David's 'house' (his dynasty) who was blameless, without spot or blemish, who rules us with unadulterated love and justice.

Can you use this psalm to pray for your nation's leaders and also for all the areas in which you have the opportunity to exercise leadership?

[1] Josh 24:15

BIBLE IN A YEAR: **Esther 4,5; Luke 11**

Where'er the Sun...

'But as for me, it is good to be near God. I have made the Sovereign LORD my refuge; I will tell of all your deeds.'[1]

God is the Holy One of Israel (v 17). He is also the Lord Almighty (vs 16,21,23,24,26,33,34), whose jurisdiction is not restricted to Israel. His rule and the scope of his accountability extends to *all* nations, hence 'woe's both for Israel (vs 1–4) and Assyria (vs 5–19). His holiness brings expectations of everyone associated with him. In Israel he expects the excluded and isolated to be treated with dignity and respect and there will be a 'day of reckoning' (v 3). Assyria is also connected with the Lord. He has chosen Assyria to punish his people for their godlessness. He sends them to trample his people down, grinding them underfoot (v 6) – but that's not the end of the story. God can use anyone, but there are still expectations about their attitudes. The Assyrians must never assume that they are sovereign (v 8), operating with free rein. Power corrupts so easily, creating a hubris (v 12) which assumes total independence (v 13). They will be scorched by God's holiness (vs 17,18).

Isaiah takes up the remnant theme (vs 20–34) introduced in 4:2,3 and 6:13. We have seen throughout the early chapters of the prophecy how hope and judgement are linked. Here again there is hope for God's people, alongside judgement on those who have sought to destroy them. God's salvation means the destruction of evil. John's epistle reminds us that is why Jesus came, 'to destroy the devil's work'.[2] Yet, even for the people who have close association with the Holy One, there will be only a few who remain. Being linked to the Holy One of Israel carries responsibilities, just as believers in the Lord Jesus have gracious demands on their bought-with-a-price identity. However, not all who say, 'Lord, Lord' will be welcomed in the end.[3]

This chapter takes us into the field of geopolitics. Are there implications from this passage for how you think about and pray for global issues?

[1] Ps 73:28 [2] 1 John 3:8 [3] Matt 7:21

BIBLE IN A YEAR: **Esther 6,7; Luke 12**

Isaiah 11

I Won't Eat you!

Your kingdom come – and start with us here and now.

Political and business leaders cast visions of how things might be – a transformed and ideal future. They aim to lift the heart and eyes to a new era, away from the flawed present. The present for Judah is the great kingdom of David, now reduced to a stump. Human leaders' plans get derailed by peoples' weakness and unpredictability.

The Spirit of God takes this dried-up stump and creates something so fruitful that our hearts leap in anticipation. The same Spirit produces a wise decision-maker. Decisions that derive from the fear of the Lord mean that power does not oppress but blesses the needy and the poor (v 4). How we treat people whose needs are easily ignored is always a marker of the Spirit's ministry in us. It is a sign of the healing of relationships that he brings (vs 6–9), with both internal and external hostility overcome (v 13).

In politics, a focus on the future is often ultimately disappointing. Isaiah's vision is built on the unbreakable promises of God. His vision is enhanced for us in the signs of their fulfilment in the Lord Jesus. He uses weak things to shame the strong. He smashes barriers between peoples, creating peace through his cross and uniting them in his love. He brings people home from every nation, protecting them to the end. We pray 'your kingdom come'; and, as we feed the poor, work against discrimination, forgive and strive for unity, we express the desire to see that future kingdom displayed in our present communities.

What's your vision for the future? Has your church prayerfully considered how that vision impacts your engagement with the community today?

BIBLE IN A YEAR: **Esther 8–10; Luke 13**

Devoted to Praise

'Blest be the everlasting God, the Father of our Lord; be his abounding mercy praised, his majesty adored.'[1]

I recently attended Praise Gathering, with a four-hundred-strong choir singing praise songs. In a troubled world, it might seem self-indulgent for hundreds of Christians to devote hours to enjoying themselves in a night of praise. Isaiah 12 inserts itself into a very troubled story. It reminds us that sometimes it's right to set aside everything else that could rightly occupy our time and focus purely on celebrating God's goodness. The passage sparks off thoughts of the song of Moses, Mary's song and psalms of praise,[2] extravagant expressions of thanks for God's intervention and victory. This song is sung, 'In that day' (v 1), the day when God's promises are seen to come to fulfilment. The day when justified anger is blessedly now turned away and replaced by comfort; when peace is established, a permanent peace, because the Lord himself is Saviour and Defender. God's 'salvation' (vs 2 (twice), 3) is the great theme: salvation that provides an antidote to fear, a defence against enemies and a fullness of joy.

We continually need reminders of salvation. Baptism, communion and Christian fellowship (modelling God's forgiveness and love) are just three. Communion is both a reminder to us and a proclamation of the Lord's death to others. Praise is never solely internal. If the Holy One of Israel is among us it begets an overspill of praise. What God does in Zion does not stay in Zion! It becomes a witness to all nations, calling others to join in exalting him (vs 4,5). When others seek to demean God and the church, our call is to witness to our experience of him and to talk up the way we have been blessed by his people. We must not be quiet about what God has done. Our role is to make his greatness known, way beyond the bounds of his people.

How can you encourage other believers to praise and non-believers to hear about God's great works?

---

[1] 'Blest be the everlasting God', Isaac Watts (1674-1748) [2] Deut 32; Luke 1:46–55

BIBLE IN A YEAR: **Job 1,2; Psalm 80**

Isaiah 13

They are not the Greatest

Thank you, our Father, that in shaking the heaven and the earth you gift us a kingdom that cannot be shaken.[1]

What does Babylon stand for? It's the jewel of the kingdoms, a place of glory (v 19). In today's world, we might see the names of fashionable cities appearing on high-class carrier bags. You'd be proud to call them home. Babylon represents the pinnacle of human achievement, which easily becomes vaunting pride (vs 11,12). In the book of Revelation, Babylon symbolises everything ungodly about humanity, setting itself up as a challenge to God and his power. Effectively, it is an alternative kingdom, a counterweight to God's rule. These kingdoms in our world, whether places like the Roman empire, the Third Reich and the Soviet Union, or dominions like consumerism and materialism, look invulnerable. It seems they will last for ever – but there is a day, the day of the Lord (vs 6,9), which will bring destruction, ending the abuse of power and the domination of the rich and powerful. We believe there will be a final day of the Lord which will eradicate sin and evil, but we also believe there will be signs or portents of that day throughout history. The Babylonians will be overthrown by the militaristic Medes (v 17), signalling future and final victory. The Lord has access to unlimited forces to carry out his judgement (vs 4,5) and no kingdom can stand against him. For Israel, this prophecy brought strong reassurance when everything around them suggested otherwise. It does the same for us, as those who 'rejoice in my triumph' (v 3) and share in it.

We rejoice in the defeat of sin, even if we find ourselves struggling to identify with the severity of the ways judgement is depicted (eg vs 15,16). The totality of the demolition makes us wonder whether we have come to terms with the horror of sin.

'There is nothing of which it is more difficult to convince men than that the providence of God governs the world.'[2] What do you make of Calvin's statement?

[1] Heb 12:26–28 [2] John Calvin, *Isaiah*, p406–407

BIBLE IN A YEAR: **Job 3,4; Luke 14**

Knocked off Top Spot

'Rise up, Judge of the earth; pay back to the proud what they deserve.'[1]

Many of us find it difficult to integrate expressions of God's judgement into our thinking about God and the world. We readily respond positively to God's renewal. We rejoice in the divine compassion that transforms a deceiver like 'Jacob' (v 1) to create 'Israel'. We identify with the restoration of his people and we glory in the 'foreigners' who join them. However, as Isaiah constantly argues, judgement and restoration are not separate and opposite elements. They go together. Salvation comes through judgement of sin and death and the devil. Rescue necessitates defeat of powers that hold us (v 3). None of us sit comfortably with the idea of children slaughtered (v 21), Assyrians crushed (v 25) or Philistines destroyed by famine (v 30). However, all of us (even materialists and atheists) want to see right triumph, oppression stopped in its tracks and wicked powers overthrown (vs 4–6). There is rejoicing when judgement delivers lands 'at rest and at peace' (v 7) and when God's people are set free from oppression (v 25).

Judgement comes when humans set themselves up as demi-gods (vs 13–15). They act as if they hold divine power, making themselves equal with God, if not greater. It does not take much imagination to take Isaiah's scathing analysis of their pride-ridden rule and apply it to our world. World history is replete with examples of people (almost exclusively men) who have exalted themselves to *de facto* divinity. God will not brook such rivalry, especially as it results in human and ecological tragedy (vs 20). He brings humiliation on these rulers. They die and their grandeur dies with them (v 11); they are denied a proper burial place (vs 19,20) and their lineage is cut off (v 21). We heed the warnings around abuse of power and overweening pride. Our comfort is that these will be thwarted.

Where do you see the indicators of the sins of Isaiah 14 in our contemporary world? You long for God's judgement to be exercised. How do you express that?

[1] Ps 94:2

BIBLE IN A YEAR: **Job 5,6; Luke 15**

Isaiah 15,16

Weep and Wail

Give thanks that God is 'kind to the ungrateful and wicked' and pray that you will be 'merciful just as your Father is merciful'.[1]

The message of judgement now confronts Moab, but the reason for judgement remains the same: arrogant superiority and accumulated wealth (15:7). The end result will leave Moab despised and feeble (16:14). Judah's tense interactions with these distant relatives and near neighbours went back a long way.[2] It is important that they hear these words as reassurance against the threat of Moab but not as any cause for gloating. Were they so different from their neighbours? Should they not take pity on homeless refugees (one possible interpretation of 16:4)? Let's not be too quick to rush to judgement.

The Moabites are left unprotected, open and vulnerable to attack – and the attack is uncompromising, touching everyone (*every* head, *every* beard, *all* wail, 15:2,3), causing even tough army types to lose heart and cry out for help (v 4). Throughout these passages, the impact is on the environment as well as on people (15:6) and is geographically widespread (15:8,9). It is a picture of devastation; a cause for lament, where joy and gladness are a memory; a land without music (16:10). We feel the sadness for enemies in distress. We live in the tension of lamenting for people caught up in conflict, while rejoicing in the bringing down of a God-challenging regime. We always live in hope. Rebellion like this, and its judgement, will not go on for ever. There is an end to the judgement and another type of kingdom will take shape: a Davidic kingdom built on justice and righteousness (16:5). It's the only hope for Moab and for us! Oppressive regimes must be dismantled – but there is always a word of hope.

Who is 'Moab' in your situation? Having reflected on these chapters, how do you think, pray and talk about these people or institutions?

[1] Luke 6:35,36 [2] See Gen 19:30–38; Num 22–25

BIBLE IN A YEAR: **Job 7,8; Psalms 81,82**

Fragility and Eternity

God of all comfort, who comforts us in all our troubles, hear our prayer and answer our cries. We trust your timing, as we cling to your promises.

Psalm 100 provides us with words to express gratitude. This psalm enables us to express distress, although it will also help us to view our lament in a context of hope. There are times when we feel abandoned. We feel our own mortality keenly as we wither away inside. Troubled day and night, we feel unheard, and there are people criticising us. Worst of all, God does not seem to hear us. We perceive God's wrath in our circumstances (v 10). Life is falling apart for the psalmist, and the anguish is not just personal. It chimes with, and may be caused by, feelings about Zion. The psalmist loves the city of Jerusalem because it is (or has been) the place of God's glory. The mix of personal affliction and a sense of deep grief for the spiritual malaise of God's people makes for a perfect storm. Do we perhaps identify more with the personal than the corporate lament? Whatever, it's heavy sometimes to be a believer.

'But God' (see v 12) is a New Testament transition from darkness to light.[1] Here the psalmist gives his heart reasons for hope, with reminders of God's perpetual reign and his compassionate listening ear. God will never change. He is the Lord who has made promises that we can cling to, promises that secure his listening, healing and restoring. The repeated 'you will' and 'will' (see vs 13,15,16,21,26,27) exude optimistic confidence as the psalmist considers a future in which God will be glorified. This must not go unreported (v 18). The lament of the psalmist is real and not to be minimised. It is echoed by compatriots (perhaps in exile) who are like prisoners on death row (v 20). These are real feelings, not easily dismissed, but the trajectory must always be towards belief in a God who transforms.

The final verses of this psalm are taken up in Hebrews as words spoken 'about the Son'.[2] Use these verses to give thanks for the Lord Jesus Christ.

---

[1] Heb 1:8,10–12 [2] See, for example, Heb 1:1,2

BIBLE IN A YEAR: **Job 9,10; Luke 16**

Every Kindred and Tribe

Holy God, you are our Maker. You are our Rock and our Saviour. May we turn our eyes to you and keep them fixed there.

Rudyard Kipling's poem for Queen Victoria's Diamond Jubilee celebrated the achievements of the British Empire and included the refrain 'Lord God of Hosts, be with us ... yet, Lest we forget – lest we forget!'[1] It aimed to shatter any hint of complacency. All humanity is caught up in God's global purposes (17:12,13; 18:3). His rule is not restricted, like that of some local councillor or regional warlord. His writ covers Damascus (the Syrian capital) to the north and Cush (with its strange language, 18:2) to the south. Their accountability to God means judgement (17:3; 18:1,5,6). Nations may rage like the sea (17:12,13) but, as Jesus calmed the waves, they will be made still.[2] Israel or Jacob (the northern kingdom in coalition with Syria) must never think themselves immune from judgement. Seeking salvation in military coalition and forgetting 'God your Saviour' (17:10) has consequences.

Cities in the Bible often represent centres of defiance to God's rule. Their flattening is part of God's determination to turn people away from idolatry (17:7,8). Agricultural metaphors tell stories of harvests that leave only a remnant (17:4–6) – but at least a remnant remains; harvests that will be insignificant because the provider of every gift has been ignored (17:10,11); and a harvest where God diverts the produce elsewhere (18:5,6). In all this, God's actions in judgement are difficult to discern. He chooses not to rush, seeming to remain inactive (18:4). Don't be fooled into thinking that God is inattentive or unconcerned. He's there to be seen if you have eyes to see (18:4)! Thankfully, God's judgement always carries salvation for some. If there is a remnant of Israel (17:7), then also of Damascus (17:3) and Cush (18:7). He will have tribute from the most unlikely sources – from every tribe, language, people and nation.

Is complacency a danger for you and your church? Do you give proper place to our 'Father', recognising that he is someone who 'judges each person's work impartially'?[3]

---

[1] Rudyard Kipling, 'Recessional', 1897 [2] Matt 8:23–27 [3] 1 Pet 1:17

BIBLE IN A YEAR: **Job 11,12; Luke 17**

Wide, Wide as the Ocean

'There's a wideness in God's mercy, / like the wideness of the sea. / There's a kindness in God's justice, / which is more than liberty.'[1]

The spotlight turns onto Egypt, a nation whose very mention would flood the mind of God's people with memories of domination. However, Egypt was possibly 'a repository of ancient wisdom' and a 'resource for protection' against Assyria.[2] Egypt might just be the answer to Judah's needs. Isaiah erases any such idea by exposing the bankruptcy of Egyptian religion and wisdom and the fragility of their society. The Bible is never slow to mock idolatry as a human creation that fails to answer the big issues. It leaves people without hope and without God in the world (vs 1,3).[3] In images recalling the plagues of Egypt, we see every sector of Egyptian society impacted by loss of hope, leading to despair and dejection (vs 5–10). All the things they currently depend on are shown to be empty (vs 9,10). There are no words of wisdom, no strategic ideas about how to deliver themselves – 'There is nothing Egypt can do' (v 15). Their sense of lostness and inertia is met by the Lord's setting up an altar in the heart of Egypt (v 19), the very place where he has been least acknowledged. He will graciously make himself known to them and in their new-found humility they will cry out to God – and he will answer (vs 20,21).

The Lord does his work of striking and healing (v 22). There is always a restorative purpose in striking, always a provision for healing in the worst times of trial. All this judgement, all these woes – yet the end is blessing: blessing for Egypt, the Assyrians and Israel. The inclusive God draws together diverse nations for his blessing (v 25), foreshadowing the universal call of the gospel and the wisdom of God being displayed in the breaking down of historical divisions.

Are there people you think are, realistically, beyond redemption? Are there divisions in your church or with other churches that seem irresolvable? Does this passage make you think again?

[1] F W Faber, 1814–63 [2] John Goldingay, *Isaiah – Understanding the Bible*, Baker Books, 2001 [3] Eph 2:12

BIBLE IN A YEAR: **Job 13,14; Luke 18**

The Inevitable End

We ask, O God, that you make us like the Lord Jesus, who withstood the devil's attack and entrusted his life into your hands in full confidence of your love.

It's commonplace for smaller, less well-equipped countries to seek the military protection of larger, better-armed nations, but putting your trust in a currently dominant power (in this case Cush and Egypt) puts you at risk of going down with them if they fail. Then where are you? Stripped of your protection, you are left bereft, naked and vulnerable (20:5). You run from the king of Assyria hoping for solace in the might of the Egyptians – and they prove unreliable. There is no escape. The subtext for Israel is – you've rejected trust in God in favour of a flawed human power. Now they've gone, what's left? – nakedness and shoelessness! Paul talks about the renewing of our minds and not conforming to a worldly pattern of thinking that depends on human wisdom.[1] The call is to get on board with the continual process of learning to trust God and his Word.

It is staggering and bewildering to see mighty powers come to nothing (21:9). It is painful to watch, but watch and wait we must until Babylon falls (v 8). News of the defeat of Babylon is a word from God to his people who are feeling crushed (v 10). Sometimes that's all we have to hold on to: a word from God Almighty. The same proclamation is made in Revelation: 'Fallen is Babylon the Great'.[2] No longer can Babylon intoxicate the nations, but the watchman warns us that it isn't now plain sailing. He tells of morning light to come but not before night is endured. Both must be part of the unfolding picture. It will take time. For Isaiah it was one to three years, for us it is knowing that it is time-limited. But the splendour of opposing forces will 'come to an end' (v 16). The Lord God has spoken; none can gainsay it.

How can you encourage others in this waiting period between the present rule of ungodly powers and their demise under God's hand?

[1] Rom 12:1,2 [2] Rev 14:8

BIBLE IN A YEAR: **Job 15–17; Psalms 83,84**

Scripture Union

A legacy of love

Could you leave a gift in your will and ensure the good news of Jesus is shared with generations to come?

TO FIND OUT MORE, VISIT SU.ORG.UK/LEGACY OR CALL **01908 856120**

'...we will tell the next generation the praiseworthy deeds of the Lord, his power, and the wonders he has done.' **Psalm 78:4**

Hebrews

NEVER GIVE UP!

There is a story, perhaps fictional, about former British prime minister Winston Churchill who went to address a school assembly. He stood up and said three words, three times: 'Never give up', 'Never give up', 'Never give up'. Then he sat down. Those words could be written over Hebrews, which is an urgent pastoral letter written to a group of believers who are tempted to abandon their faith community. The author encourages them to remain faithful, for, if they don't, they risk the loss of everything.

In many ways Hebrews is an enigma. We don't know the author, the date, its place of writing or destination, and the title 'Hebrews' looks like an educated guess, first appearing around the year 200. Nevertheless, we can deduce some things. In the early church, from (present-day) Turkey to Egypt, they thought Paul wrote Hebrews; in Rome nobody thought that until the fifth century. Few people today think it was Paul. The church father Origen probably said the wisest thing about the author: as for who wrote it, only God knows. As for the date, some verses seem to indicate that the Temple was still standing and accordingly most people consider it was written before AD 70.

An ambiguous reference to Italy in 13:24 implies some connection with Rome. Until around 1875 most thought it was written to Jewish believers situated in Jerusalem. Since then, throughout the twentieth century, scholars have argued that they were in Rome. More recently, some have been suggesting Jerusalem again, and I am beginning to think it was written from Rome to Jerusalem. Jewish followers of Jesus living in Jerusalem were attracted to the ritual in the Temple, and the writer argued that since everything that ritual anticipated had been fulfilled in Jesus, they needed to put it behind them. Jesus offered himself to God as the perfect sacrifice for sins and was crucified outside Jerusalem. They were to follow him there, welcoming the reproach that involved – and to never give up.

Philip Church

Jesus, God's Exalted Son

As we begin reading Hebrews, ask God to illumine your mind by his Spirit and open your eyes to wonderful things about Jesus in this book.

The original readers of Hebrews were tempted to give up, so the writer introduces them to the exalted Lord Jesus. The opening words of the epistle differ from those of the other New Testament letters, in which the writer identifies himself and greets his readers. This writer begins by identifying his central concern: the exaltation of God's Son, whom he will later identify as Jesus.[1] This paragraph is a single sentence in Greek, which boils down to 'God has spoken in his Son' and 'the Son has sat down at the right hand of God'. Everything in the sentence is subordinate to that.

Since the same God who spoke to the ancestors through the prophets is now speaking in his Son, there is continuity.. There is also discontinuity: his former speech was 'partial and piecemeal';[2] his present speech 'in these last days' (v 2) is final. The writer believes that the Son's exaltation to God's right hand signals the beginning of the last days. His exaltation is God's final word to humanity. The messianic age has begun. The Son of God has inherited all things.

The exaltation of the Son to God's right hand is an allusion to Psalm 110:1, originally a command to the ancient Israelite king, showing that he ruled God's people with the power and authority of God. Here God's Son has obeyed this command by taking his seat at God's right hand in heaven. He rules not just ancient Israel, but the entire universe with the power and authority of God. Finally, his exaltation was 'After he had provided purification for sins' (v 3). This announces another central concern of Hebrews: Jesus is the great high priest who has dealt with our sins once and for all.

The writer later tells his readers to fix their eyes on Jesus.[3] Ask God to help you to fix your eyes on him as you go about your day.

[1] Heb 2:9 [2] FF Bruce, *The Christian Approach to the Old Testament*, second edition, IVF, 1955, p9
[3] Heb 12:2

BIBLE IN A YEAR: **Job 18,19; Luke 19**

Hebrews 1:5–14

Jesus Superior to Angels

Join today with the angels in worshipping the risen, exalted Christ.

Yesterday's reading ended with an allusion to Psalm 110:1 and concluded that Jesus' exaltation to God's right hand signalled his superiority to the angels. The measure of his superiority is the exalted name he has inherited. This is the 'name that is above every name'.[1] Today's reading is a chain of Old Testament quotations establishing that.

There is enough here for a week's readings, so we can only scratch the surface. The quotations begin and end with a rhetorical question, 'To which of the angels did God ever say …?' (vs 5,13), implying that God only spoke these words to his exalted Son and not to angels. Several quotations are from psalms originally spoken to the Israelite king, including the first and the last.[2] Psalm 110:1 is also reflected in verse 3, where the Son is seated at God's right hand. King David ruled God's people with the power and authority of God.

What I call 'ancient Near Eastern royal court hyperbole' has now found its true fulfilment in the risen Christ, who rules the entire universe with that same power and authority.

The third quotation and its introduction (v 6) are complex, but 'firstborn' reflects Psalm 89:27, where it is implied that God announced he would make the son of David, the firstborn, the ruler of the kings of the earth. This verse is not about the birth of Jesus but, along with the rest of the chapter, it is about his exaltation to God's right hand, his introduction to the world to come[3] as ruler of the kings of the earth. Since Jesus is now reigning over all things, we live in the overlap of the ages. We live in the present evil age, but the age to come is already here.

If the age to come is already here, how should we conduct ourselves in the present evil age?[4]

---

[1] Phil 2:9–11 [2] Pss 2:7; 110:1 [3] See Heb 2:5 [4] See, for example, Rom 13:11,12

BIBLE IN A YEAR: **Job 20,21; Luke 20**

Why Angels?

Worship Jesus, now crowned with glory and honour at God's right hand.

Today we discover why the writer thought it important to emphasise Jesus' superiority to the angels. The chapter gives three reasons, two of which are in today's reading. Verses 1–4 are the first warning passage of Hebrews, referring to the message spoken through angels. These words reflect an ancient Jewish tradition that the Law of Moses was mediated by angels.[1] If violations of the Law (mediated by angels) received just punishment, how much more serious is it for those who neglect the gospel of salvation declared by the Lord?

The second reason is in verses 5–9, a meditation on Psalm 8:4–6. In the Greek Old Testament (which the writer always quotes) these verses refer to humans being both a little lower than the angels and crowned with glory and honour, having been given dominion over all God's handiwork. Psalm 8 is Genesis 1 set to music, celebrating humanity's dignity as made in the image of God.

Some think that these verses celebrate not the dignity of humanity as made in God's image, but the exaltation of Jesus,[2] but I think the TNIV has it right – the verses are about human dignity (vs 5–8) *and* Jesus' exaltation (v 9). The section begins by claiming that dominion over the world to come has been given not to angels but to humans. Jesus enters the picture in verse 9 (the first time his name appears in Hebrews). At present we don't see humans exercising our God-given dominion, but we do see Jesus, the representative human. He was made a little lower than the angels, suffering death for everyone, and is now exalted above the angels, crowned with glory and honour, where he rules the world to come (v 5) with the power and authority of God.

Adam's role in the garden was 'to work it and take care of it'.[3] This is our calling, now and in the world to come. How are we doing?

[1] See Gal 3:19 [2] See, for example, these verses in the ESV translation [3] Gen 2:15

BIBLE IN A YEAR: **Job 22,23; Psalm 85**

Psalm 103

Praise the Lord

'Praise the LORD, my soul; all my inmost being, praise his holy name.'[1]

At the outset of this psalm, the psalmist calls upon his entire being to praise the Lord for what the Lord characteristically does for him (vs 1–5). Then the psalm looks back to the Lord's self-revelation to Moses as a compassionate and gracious God (vs 6–9). After that, it moves out in ever-widening circles to celebrate what God does for his people (vs 10–14), for all humanity (vs 15–18), until, finally, the whole creation comes into view (v 19). It then turns to the supernatural world, calling on the angels (vs 20,21) and all creation (v 22) to praise the Lord. The psalm closes as it opens, encouraging the psalmist to add his voice to the praise of the universe, like the single note of a triangle penetrating the sound of an orchestra in full flight.

Many psalms celebrate God's great deeds in the past, what God has done for his people. In this psalm, the past is muted at best, amid all the present-tense verbs. The psalm celebrates what God is like – his settled attitude of compassion, not only towards an individual, not only towards his people and, indeed, not only towards all humanity, but towards the whole created universe.

Different verses in the psalm will stand out to different readers. For me, verses 11 and 12, in the centre of the psalm, are a high point: 'as high as the heavens are above the earth, so great is his love for those who fear him; as far as the east is from the west, so far has he removed our transgressions from us.' For those with a personal relationship with the covenant God, especially those who revere his name, his love and his forgiveness are immeasurable.

Go through the psalm again and find the verse (or verses) that are your high point for today. Commit them to memory and carry them with you through the day.

[1] Ps 103:1

BIBLE IN A YEAR: **Job 24–26; Luke 21**

Jesus Became One of Us

Lord, give me an open ear to hear your voice in the Scriptures today.

Verse 16 contains the last reference to angels in these first two chapters: 'For surely it is not angels he helps, but Abraham's descendants' (v 16). They explain why Jesus had to become fully human. God planned to bring many sons and daughters to glory through Jesus, the pioneer of our salvation – the one who blazed the trail for us and is now crowned with glory and honour. To do that, he needed to identify with those sons and daughters in every way, including their suffering. This identification was so close that he refers to them as his brothers and sisters. Since Jesus came to redeem his brothers and sisters rather than the angels, he didn't become an angel: he became one of us.

He did this so that he could become a 'merciful and faithful high priest in service to God' (v 17). Aside from a hint in Hebrews 1:3 about Jesus making atonement for sins, this is the first explicit reference to the theme that will occupy the writer in chapters 5–10: Jesus is our great high priest. As Alexander Nairne wrote over a hundred years ago, it was as though the author was saying, 'Think of him as a priest and I can make you understand'.[1]

The writer draws two implications here about Jesus, the merciful and faithful high priest. He was faithful to God in the past when he offered himself as a sacrifice of atonement to deal with our sins, and he is merciful to us now in his ongoing ministry before God. Since he was tempted as we are and suffered in that temptation, he can help us when we are tempted. These two aspects of the work of Jesus will be gradually unpacked as the letter proceeds.

References to suffering imply that the readers were enduring suffering and were tempted to give up. Pray today for those who suffer hardship for Jesus, wherever they are.

[1] Alexander Nairne, *The Epistle to the Hebrews*, Cambridge University Press, 1922, plxviii

BIBLE IN A YEAR: **Job 27,28; Luke 22**

Hebrews 3

Encourage One Another

Lord, speak into my life by your Holy Spirit today as I read the Scriptures.

This chapter has two parts: a comparison between Jesus and Moses, and a warning from the example of the wilderness generation. There are also two unusual conditional sentences, where our status in the present will be disclosed in the future. The first is in verse 6, concluding six verses containing the word 'house' six times. The word is ambiguous and only at the end do we discover that 'house' means 'household': we are God's household now if we persevere into the future, firmly holding our confidence and hope.

In chapters 1 and 2 we overheard God and Jesus speaking to one another in the Scriptures. Now, the Holy Spirit speaks, addressing God's people. The Spirit quotes Psalm 95:7–11, where God warned the people worshipping[1] not to be like the faithless wilderness generation who were excluded from the resting place God had prepared for them in the Promised Land.[2] They were unable to enter because of unbelief, and the writer of Hebrews emphasises that readers of the epistle need to persevere in faith to the very end, demonstrating that they truly have come to share in Christ (the other conditional sentence, v 14).

The Spirit applied words that were first spoken to the Temple worshippers, to the readers of Hebrews and, since it is still 'Today' (v 15), the Spirit now applies them to us. In verses 12 and 13 we hear the Spirit calling us, not so much to look out for ourselves but to look out for others. We are to encourage one another so that no member of our believing communities is hardened by the deceitfulness of sin and so excluded from God's ultimate rest, the glory to which God is bringing us.[3]

Verses 12 and 13 are a warning against temptation. As you gather with others, be on the lookout for a sister or brother who needs your help to persevere.

[1] See Ps 95:1–7 [2] See Deut 12:9 for this imagery [3] Heb 2:10

BIBLE IN A YEAR: **Job 29,30; Luke 23**

A Rest for God's People

Lord, give me the grace to listen carefully to what you are saying to me today.

In these verses the writer of Hebrews moves away from the application of Psalm 95 as a warning to the faithless wilderness generation and applies the same psalm as a promise to his readers. Verses 1–11 begin and end with exhortation, 'let us be careful' (v 1) and 'Let us … make every effort' (v 11). Both exhortations are about entering God's rest, still available to the people of God. We are to be careful that none of us misses out on God's rest, as we make every effort to enter it.

In English, as in Greek and Hebrew, the word 'rest' can be a state of rest or a resting place and at times this chapter seems to move between the two. I think the dominant idea is of a resting place. In the psalm and in Hebrews 3, the faithless wilderness generation were excluded from the Promised Land. Now, however, God is no longer leading his people to the Promised Land: he is leading us to glory.[1] This is the resting place God entered at the creation[2] and where Jesus is seated at God's right hand. It is this resting place that remains available to the people of God. But we must make every effort not to miss out by following the example of the disobedient wilderness generation.

Verses 12 and 13 are often applied to the Bible, but I think it is more than that. The verses conclude the section that began in 3:7 with the Holy Spirit speaking to us through the Scriptures, bringing to mind what Hebrews 1:1–2 has already said about God speaking to us through his exalted Son. The Word of God is what God is saying to us by his Spirit and through his exalted Son. We are to pay close attention.[3]

The writer wants nobody to fall away. Are there people in your sphere of influence whom you can pray for and encourage today lest they fall away?

[1] Heb 2:10 [2] Gen 2:1–3 [3] Heb 2:1

BIBLE IN A YEAR: **Job 31,32; Psalms 86,87**

Hebrews 4:14 – 5:10

A Priest Like Melchizedek

Come to the throne of grace with confidence today and receive mercy and grace to meet your need.

Having twice referred to Jesus as a high priest,[1] now the writer establishes this both from Scripture and from the readers' understanding of priesthood. He begins by reminding them of three things: a high priest needs to be one of the people, beset with similar weaknesses; a high priest is appointed to represent the people in things related to God, offering gifts and sacrifices for his sins; and a high priest is not self-appointed, but is appointed by God.

Then he turns to Jesus. Jesus was appointed by God when God, who spoke Psalm 2:7 to him, also spoke Psalm 110:4 to him: 'You are a priest for ever, in the order of Melchizedek'. Jesus offered prayers to God, who was able to save him from death (in chapters 8–10 he will explain Jesus' offering for sins); and Jesus was one of us, learning (the cost of) obedience from his sufferings. He concludes that when God heard the cries of Jesus and saved him from death (in the resurrection), Jesus became the source of eternal salvation for all who obey him.

Hebrews 4:14–16 introduces Hebrews 5–10 and explains some implications from understanding Jesus as our great high priest. Because he shares our human nature and was tempted in every way as we are – and more, since he did not sin – he can sympathise with our weakness. This gives us encouragement to approach God's throne of grace in prayer and receive mercy and grace in our time of need, especially when we are tempted to loosen our hold on our faith. God's presence is freely open to us at any time. Our confidence to approach God comes from having a great high priest who understands our weakness and appears in the presence of God on our behalf.

We approach God in prayer not only for ourselves, but also for others. Spend some time praying for those you know who need God's mercy and grace today.

[1] Heb 2:17; 3:1

BIBLE IN A YEAR: **Job 33,34; Luke 24**

Us, Them and You

Ask God to strengthen the faith and hear the cries of those facing persecution for their faith in places where it is difficult to live as a follower of Jesus.

Today we come to a very difficult passage. The book of Hebrews is no mere dispassionate treatise on the theology of priesthood; rather, it is an urgent pastoral communication to people in danger of abandoning their faith. The writer has introduced Jesus as a high priest like Melchizedek. He wants to say more, but feels that he cannot because his readers are no longer trying to understand. He encourages them to progress from milky basics to solid food and does so with a strong warning.

The first three paragraphs (in the NIV) of chapter 6 use three different pronouns. The first paragraph is about 'us'. He identifies with them and encourages them move forward with him to maturity. The second paragraph is about 'those' people who, from the descriptions in verses 4 and 5, appear to be believers in Jesus who are tempted to fall away. Should they do so, it is impossible, he says, to restore them to repentance, since what they are doing is tantamount to crucifying the Son of God again. The third paragraph is about 'you'. He is confident that his readers are on the way to salvation, for he has seen their work in the past and their love for God's people. Consequently, he encourages them to persevere diligently to the very end.

The Christian life can be difficult, especially for those experiencing persecution and harassment for their faith. There will be times when we are all tempted to give up. The writer stops short of saying that those addressed in Hebrews had given up and cannot be restored. He does, however, give a very strong warning about the impossibility of restoration for any who might.

This difficult text seems to contradict verses such as John 10:27–30. Hebrews 6 and John 10 are both part of Scripture. How can we hold them in tension?

BIBLE IN A YEAR: **Job 35,36; Philippians 1**

Two Unchangeable Things

Ask God to give you hearing ears to hear his Word to you today and to let it discern your thoughts and attitudes.

The last Greek word in verse 12 is 'promises',[1] a noun that appears twice in these verses alongside the verb 'to promise'. God's promise to Abraham is one of the unchangeable things. The other one is God's oath. After Abraham and Isaac returned from Abraham's would-be sacrifice of Isaac, God reiterated his earlier promise of numerous descendants and blessing for the nations and, to make it doubly sure, he confirmed the promise with an oath.[2]

The point of this example appears in verse 18. Abraham persevered with faith and patience and ultimately received what God had promised. His example is given to encourage the readers (and that includes us) firmly to take hold of the hope set before us, that is the hope of entering God's rest.[3] This hope is sure, because it is anchored in Jesus who has entered God's throne room as our forerunner on our behalf and is seated at the right hand of God. That Jesus is our forerunner indicates that eventually, with faith and patience, we shall receive what God has promised and attain to God's rest.

One way to help us understand this rather complex and strange-sounding argument is to remember that the readers of Hebrews were facing persecution and were tempted to give up. While the writer was confident about their faithfulness, he still needed to encourage them to persevere. He drew his encouragement from the faith of Abraham, who received what God had promised, from the example of Jesus, who endured suffering and is now exalted in God's presence, and from God, who cannot lie. Our God is the God who cannot lie, who makes promises (and sometimes confirms them with an oath). Our God is faithful and will always give what he has promised.

Ask God to fill the hearts and minds of those who are called to suffer for the name of Jesus with hope in our promise-keeping God.

[1] NIV translates it as a verb [2] Gen 22:15–18 [3] Heb 4:6–11

BIBLE IN A YEAR: **Job 37,38; Psalm 88**

Creation Then and Now

'LORD my God, you are very great; you are clothed with splendour and majesty.'[1]

This psalm looks like parts of Genesis 1 set to music, as it celebrates God's creative activity, past and present. It also weaves together words about God ('he' statements) and words addressed to God ('you' statements). It opens and closes with the psalmist calling on himself to praise the Lord, and then divides into five parts. Verses 1–5 celebrate the greatness of God, who set the earth on its immovable foundations. Verses 6–18 meditate on Genesis 1:6,7, where God set limits on the water. Verses 19–23 meditate on Genesis 1:16–18, where God created sun and moon. Verses 24–30 acknowledge that God sustains all creatures. Verses 31–35 close the psalm with a prayer that the Lord's glory will endure and the psalmist's resolve to sing to the Lord all his life. In this psalm, humans are also God's creatures and there is no hint that we are made in God's image or have dominion (we learn that elsewhere in the Bible). God's covenant people are also conspicuously absent.

Whereas Genesis 1 simply states that God set limits on the water, this psalm describes the ongoing benefits of life-giving water from God the 'celestial sprinkler'.[2] Whereas Genesis 1 tells of God creating sun and moon to rule day and night, the psalm celebrates the rhythms of life with the flow of the seasons and alternating day and night. Verses 24–30 celebrate in delightful detail how all creatures depend on God, as we, along with the non-human creation, look to God to provide our needs at the proper time. Truly, when the Lord opens his hand, he satisfies us with good things (v 28). Appropriately, the last line of the psalm calls on us to add our praise to the psalmist's.

This psalm is about the world that God 'so loved'.[3] May we hear the challenge to love God's world ourselves and learn to care for it as God does.

[1] Ps 104:1 [2] John Goldingay, *Psalms 90–150*, Baker Academic, 2006, p187 [3] John 3:16

BIBLE IN A YEAR: **Job 39,40; Philippians 2**

What about Melchizedek?

Boldly approach the throne of grace through Jesus, our great high priest, and find grace and mercy to help you in your time of need.[1]

Melchizedek appears only twice in the Old Testament.[2] The writer of Hebrews has already claimed three times that Jesus is a priest for ever after the order of Melchizedek, quoting Psalm 110:4.[3] Now he shows how a Melchizedek priest is superior to a Levite priest, something he does from the events recounted in Genesis 14. He tells the story and explains its significance, using arguments that seem strange to us but would have made sense to his original readers.

In verses 1–3 he says some things about the meaning of the name Melchizedek and explains that his sudden appearance and disappearance in Genesis without parents, a genealogy, or any record of his death (when many people in Genesis have all three) means that he lives for ever. He also notes that Melchizedek blessed Abraham and that Abraham gave him a tenth of the spoils of the battle recounted in the preceding verses. In verses 4–10 he concludes that, because a greater person blesses a lesser person, Melchizedek was greater than Abraham. Because Abraham gave him a tenth of the spoils, that means that Levi, Abraham's as yet unborn descendant, gave Melchizedek the tenth. He concludes that Melchizedek is greater than Levi and therefore a Melchizedek priest is greater than a Levite priest.

Notice, meanwhile, the end of verse 3. He is discussing Melchizedek, but he really wants to say things about Jesus so he compares the two, but not as we might expect. Jesus doesn't resemble Melchizedek – Melchizedek resembles Jesus. 'Just think how great he was', he says in verse 4, but the implication of verse 3 is that, when compared with Jesus, his greatness fades away.

This is perhaps the most difficult chapter in Hebrews. Ask God to enlighten your mind by his Spirit and help you understand what God is saying through today's and tomorrow's readings.

[1] Cf Heb 4:14–16 [2] Gen 14:17–20; Ps 110:4 [3] Heb 5:6,10; 6:20

BIBLE IN A YEAR: **Job 41,42; Philippians 3**

A Priest For Ever

'Before the throne of God above / I have a strong and perfect plea; / a great High Priest whose name is Love, / who ever lives and pleads for me.'[1]

This section is in two parts. Verses 11–25 establish that Jesus is a superior priest to the Levite priests and verses 26–28 summarise all that has been said about Jesus the high priest until now and introduce chapters 8–10 dealing with his ongoing ministry. While Jesus is seated at God's right hand, he also ministers in God's presence on our behalf.

In verses 11–25, the Genesis Melchizedek story fades into the background and Psalm 110:4 returns. The writer concentrates on the term 'for ever' and God's oath that guarantees it. Jesus is a priest for ever. Unlike those other priests who die and need to be replaced, his life is 'indestructible' (v 16). He lives for ever and has a permanent priesthood, something that God has guaranteed with an oath. God will never change his mind about Jesus. If the argument is complex, the conclusion is not: 'Jesus … is able to save completely those who come to God through him, because he always lives to intercede for them' (vs 24,25). Take hold of this today.

The summary in verses 26–28 lists some of his qualities: he is 'holy, blameless, pure, set apart from sinners, exalted above the heavens'. Verse 27 introduces a phrase that will become important in chapters 9–10: 'once for all'. Here we learn that, unlike the Levite priests, Jesus does not need to offer daily animal sacrifices for his own sins and those of the people. He made his offering once for all when he offered not an animal but himself. His is a sacrifice that never needs to be repeated. For that reason, he truly meets our need. God will never change his mind about those who believe in Jesus.

Jesus' sacrifice can never be repeated. Look again at Hebrews 6:6. Think about the importance of persevering and thank God for Jesus' ministry, enabling you to persevere.

[1] Charitie Lees Bancroft, 1841–1923

BIBLE IN A YEAR: **Proverbs 1,2; Philippians 4**

Hebrews 8

Jesus' Superior Ministry

Thank God for the forgiveness you have because of the death of Jesus in your place.

In verse 1, the writer refers to Psalm 110:1 for a second time, repeating his earlier claim that Jesus sat down at the right hand of God's throne. This implies that he rules the universe with the power and authority of God. There is something else, though, that is initially counterintuitive. As we noticed yesterday, Jesus lives for ever to intercede for us. Although he has sat down in God's presence, he has an ongoing ministry. This is the subject of this chapter.

The writer compares Jesus' ministry with that of the priests in the Temple or tabernacle and shows it to be superior on two counts. First, his ministry is in a superior sanctuary not made by human hands. Those human-built sanctuaries are symbolic, pointing to the true sanctuary built by God. Second, his ministry is superior because he is mediator of a superior covenant, the new covenant prophesied by Jeremiah.[1] Verses 8–12 contain the longest Old Testament quotation in the New, introduced and concluded with two remarkable statements. That God announced a new covenant implies that there is something lacking in the old one (v 7) and, more starkly, by calling it 'new', God has made the first one obsolete (v 13).

The problem with the old covenant was that the people could not keep it – they did not remain faithful. The benefits of the new one include, first, God's writing his laws not on stone but on our hearts and, second, God's promise, 'I ... will remember their sins no more' (v 12). Forgetting is a human weakness to which God is not subject. God does not forget our sins; rather, he wills to remember them no more. Once forgiven, they will never be brought up again.

This chapter brings new significance to part of the Old Testament. Take some time now to think through the implications of this. The exaltation of Jesus changes everything.

[1] Jer 31:31–34

BIBLE IN A YEAR: **Proverbs 3,4; Psalm 89**

Tabernacle Service

'Enter his gates with thanksgiving and his courts with praise; give thanks to him and praise his name.'[1]

These verses explain the suggestion in Hebrews 8 that Temple and Tabernacle worship was in some way symbolic of the work of Christ. The first paragraph describes the shape of the wilderness tabernacle and the second describes its ritual. It is important to note the play on the words 'first' and 'new' (or 'second'), introduced in 8:7,13 and appearing several times in today's reading. Sometimes (8:7,13; 9:1,8) they have a temporal sense and sometimes (9:2,3,6,7) they have a spatial sense.[2]

The tabernacle and its ritual, with things happening daily in the first (outer) tent and annually in the second (inner) tent, symbolically anticipate the time of the new order. Since the second tent was situated within the first, a reader encountering verse 8 for the first time might be tempted to think that the second tent was hidden away from view by the first,[3] but the reference to the time of new order in verse 10 shows that the temporal sense is back. The Most Holy Place of verse 8 is the true tent of 8:1,2 and the way into it was not disclosed while the tabernacle was functioning. The (first) tabernacle's role was symbolic, anticipating the new covenant ministry of Jesus that would ultimately come to pass.

Tabernacle worship was an important part of God's revelation of himself to his people, as Exodus 25:8 shows ('make a sanctuary for me, and I will dwell among them'). The reason it was so important was that it anticipated how God would eventually dwell with his people in Christ. Now that he has been exalted to God's right hand and the new covenant has been inaugurated, the reality has come and the symbols have been abolished. We have open access to God's presence.

The torn Temple curtain[4] symbolises the truth explained here. Thank God for the welcome we now have in his presence through the death of Jesus.

---

[1] Ps 100:4 [2] 'Outer' and 'inner' in vs 6,7 are 'first' and 'second' in Greek [3] 'Tabernacle' (v 8) is the same word in Greek as 'tent' [4] Mark 15:38

BIBLE IN A YEAR: **Proverbs 5,6; Colossians 1**

Comprehensive Salvation

Lord Jesus, thank you that you came to do away with sin by sacrificing yourself. Cleanse my heart as I come into your presence today.

These verses deal with past, present and future salvation. Yesterday's reading referred to tabernacle worship and, in particular, the annual entrance of the high priest into the most holy place on the Day of Atonement. Today's reading emphasises the contrast between that regularly repeated ritual and the single, unique, once only, entrance of Christ into the 'greater and more perfect tabernacle ... not made with human hands' (v 11) – that is, his entrance into 'heaven itself' (v 24). Rather than offering animal blood, he 'offered himself unblemished to God' (v 14). The writer uses a 'how much more' argument. If the former offerings brought outward cleansing, 'How much more' (v 14) will the blood of Christ bring inner, conscience cleansing.

The writer has twice claimed that Jesus sat down in the presence of God.[1] Here he says something more. While Jesus is seated at God's right hand, ruling the universe with the power and authority of God, he is there in God's presence for us, with an ongoing ministry of intercession (v 24).[2] Jesus offered himself to God for us in the past, he appears in God's presence for us in the present and the chapter concludes stating that he will appear a second time to bring salvation to those who are waiting for him (v 28).

Christ's comprehensive saving work in the past, the present and the future has consequences for us. He offered himself once to God in the past to cleanse our consciences and, so that we may serve the living God, he continually intercedes for us in the present, to strengthen us when tempted. The expectation of his second appearance in the future reminds us that our final salvation is still to come, calling us to persevere as we await his appearance.

We are urged to be active in God's service, approaching the 'throne of grace[3] when tested and focusing on Christ's second appearing for final salvation. How do we measure up?

[1] Heb 1:3; 8:1 [2] See also Heb 4:14–16; 7:25 [3] Heb 4:16

BIBLE IN A YEAR: **Proverbs 7,8; Colossians 2**

A Sacrifice for All

Lord Jesus, take my life and let it be consecrated to you this day.[1]

The writer of Hebrews likes the expression 'once for all', using it five times. We encountered it twice in yesterday's reading, it appears twice in these verses and once in chapter 7.[2] Four times he connects the expression with the sacrifice of Christ, making his point that this sacrifice is unique, once only and never to be repeated. The other time is when he contrasts Christ's unique sacrifice with the former sacrifices that were repeated 'endlessly year after year' (v 1). If they had been effective, he asks, 'would not they have stopped being offered?' (v 2). For, then, the worshippers would have been cleansed 'once for all' and the sacrifices would no longer be necessary. His point is that the repetition of those sacrifices shows that they were ineffective.

Reflecting on Psalm 40:6–8, the writer shows why the sacrifice of Christ was effective when the former sacrifices were not. Encoded into the Old Testament was the understanding that animal sacrifices were insufficient to atone for sin in any lasting way, especially when offered superficially. What God desires is the freely offered submission of the will, seen in the climax of the psalm quotation, 'I have come to do your will, my God' (v 7). When Jesus came into the world (v 5), he announced in words taken from this psalm that he was coming to do God's will.[3]

The verses indicate that, for Jesus, doing God's will involved the offering of his body. We need to take care, however, not to reduce the will of God for Jesus to the cross alone. His death was the culmination of an entire life freely offered to God. To do God's will, whatever that involved, was what made his death on the cross effective in making us holy.

Jesus offered his will completely to God. God calls us to do the same. Make this the subject of your prayers today.

[1] From Frances R Havergal, 1836–79, 'Take my life and let it be' [2] See Heb 7:27; 9:12,26; 10:2,10
[3] John 6:38

BIBLE IN A YEAR: **Proverbs 9,10; Psalm 90**

Psalm 105

Redeemed for What?

'Give praise to the Lord, call on his name; make known ... what he has done ... sing his praises; tell of all his wonderful acts.'[1]

The first book of Chronicles quotes part of this psalm, relating how David appointed it to be sung when the Ark of the Covenant arrived in Jerusalem.[2] Since Chronicles is generally dated to the Exile, it shows how this psalm was relevant then. Verses 1–11 call on God's people to praise him and remember his great deeds, the covenant with Abraham and the promise of the land. Verses 12–44 summarise the story from Abraham to Joshua, showing how God repeatedly acted on his people's behalf and ultimately fulfilled that promise by giving them the land. Take another look and notice all the verses beginning with 'He' (the Lord).

These verses deal with the patriarchs in Canaan (vs 12–16), the captivity in Egypt (vs 17–38) and the Exodus and wilderness wanderings (vs 39–43). Significant for the exiles in Babylon are the 22 verses telling of God's activity during the captivity in Egypt. If God could intervene on his people's behalf in Egypt and deliver them from captivity there, he could surely do the same for them now in Babylon. The giving of the Law at Sinai and the story of their rebellion in the wilderness are conspicuous by their absence. The people went straight from Egypt to Canaan, giving hope that the exiles would soon go straight from Babylon to Judea.

Verse 45 makes up for the silence about the giving of the Law. God did these great wonders so that 'they might keep his precepts and observe his laws'. That would give the exiles something to think about. The reason they were in Babylon was that they had not done this. They had forsaken God's covenant and disobeyed his laws. Would they amend their ways?

'... we are God's handiwork, created in Christ Jesus to do good works, which God prepared ... for us to do.'[3] What good works has God prepared for you today?

[1] Ps 105:1,2, TNIV [2] 1 Chr 16:8–22 [3] Eph 2:10

BIBLE IN A YEAR: **Proverbs 11,12; Colossians 3**

Let Us Draw Near

Loving God, I open myself to you now to hear what the Holy Spirit is saying to me through the Scriptures.

Today's reading is a good example of how the writer uses Scripture quotations and their application to encourage his readers. Here he quotes Jeremiah, in which the Holy Spirit 'testifies to us' (v 15) about God's new covenant, which includes our God-given enablement to obey God's law and God's resolve not to remember our sins.[1] Then he applies that scripture and encourages his readers. He applies the testimony of the Holy Spirit through Jeremiah to Jesus' single, unique offering of himself as a sacrifice for sins. Jesus, having done this, sat down at God's right hand, awaiting the subjugation of his enemies. That he is *seated* at the right hand of God, contrasts sharply with the priests who *stand* day after day, offering sacrifices that can never take away sins. In contrast to these sacrifices, by his one sacrifice Jesus has for ever fitted us to enter God's presence.[2]

Verses 19–25 are densely packed and are difficult to deal with, but we can notice several things. There are two 'since' clauses: 'since we have confidence to enter' God's presence (v 19) and 'since we have a great priest' over God's house (v 21). There is a 'having' clause (v 22), like another 'since' clause: since we have been inwardly and outwardly cleansed. There is also a 'for' clause: 'for he who promised is faithful' (v 23). These clauses all support the three things the writer encourages them to do. He wants his readers to draw near to God with sincere hearts, to hold unswervingly to their hope and to consider how to spur one another on to good deeds. The last one is important and practical. He does not want his readers missing from the community gatherings: they need to be there, encouraging one another.

If I am not in a community of believers, how can I encourage my struggling sister or brother to persevere? Let this motivate us to continue to gather with God's people.

[1] See Jer 31:31–34 [2] This is the sense of the expression 'made perfect' (v 14)

BIBLE IN A YEAR: **Proverbs 13,14; Colossians 4**

Us, Them and You – Again

Loving God, give me the grace and persistence to persevere until the end.

Today's reading is another strong warning, this time against intentional, ongoing sin by someone who has 'received the knowledge of the truth' (v 26). That is, someone who has acknowledged the truth and validity of all that the writer has expounded in chapters 7–10 about the priesthood of Jesus and his sacrifice for sins. To deliberately continue to sin in the light of that acknowledgement is, according to verse 29, to trample the Son of God underfoot, to treat as unholy the sanctifying blood of the covenant and to insult the Spirit of grace. Such people will fall into the hands of the living God, a dreadful thing.

Let us look again at the pronouns as we did in chapter 6. 'If we deliberately keep on sinning', he begins (v 26) and he ends with 'But we [are not like that but] … have faith and are saved' (v 39). There is no suggestion that his readers are sinning in this way.

Between these two 'we' statements are a series of 'anyone' statements, describing deliberate and persistent sin, and a series of 'you' statements describing the believers themselves. You were insulted and persecuted in the past and had your property confiscated, and yet you accepted all that joyfully because you knew you had 'better and lasting possessions' (v 34). The writer concludes with a word of encouragement, 'your confidence … will be richly rewarded. You need to persevere so that … you will receive what he [God] has promised' (vs 35,36).

We need to clarify that this passage does not refer to someone 'caught in a sin' who can be restored gently.[1] This is deliberate, persistent, wilful rebellion against God, 'outright apostasy'.[2] It is equivalent to sinning 'defiantly', for which the penalty was to be 'cut off' from God's people.[3]

It is true to say that anyone worried that they may have committed such a sin, has almost certainly not – defiant sinners do not worry! Be encouraged with these words.

[1] Gal 6:1 [2] FF Bruce, *The Epistle to the Hebrews*, Eerdmans, 1990, p261 [3] Num 15:30,31

BIBLE IN A YEAR: **Proverbs 15,16; 1 Thessalonians 1**

Commended for their Faith

'I do believe; help me overcome my unbelief!'[1]

For the rest of this week we are reading Hebrews 11, that inspiring list of faithful people from the past who were selected by the writer to encourage his people. Today's reading begins with a description of faith and then lists the faithful exploits of Abel, Enoch and Noah.

The opening description refers to things hoped for and things unseen. What we hope for is clearly in the future but, as we read the chapter, we will notice that often the unseen things are also in the future. This is clear with Noah, who was warned about the coming flood, and we will also find more unseen things that people acted on over the next few days. Be on the lookout for them. However, what comes out most clearly in these opening verses is the word 'commended'. You will have read it three times as you read the verses for today (vs 2,4,5) and the Greek word for 'commended' also underlies the words 'spoke well of' in verse 4. The ancients were commended for their faith, Abel was commended as righteous when God commended his offerings and Enoch was commended as one who pleased God.

These verses also contain some 'we' statements. It is faith that enables us to be confident about what we hope for and assured about what we do not see. It is faith that enables us to believe that God commanded the universe into existence. By earnestly seeking God, we can also have ourselves included in the 'anyone' statement of verse 6. It is faith that enables us to believe that God exists and it is faith that enables us earnestly to seek him, knowing that when we seek him in this way he will reward us.

'Ask and it will be given to you; seek and you will find'.[2] As we consider Hebrews 11, be prepared to seek God earnestly and so receive God's commendation.

[1] Mark 9:24 [2] Matt 7:7

BIBLE IN A YEAR: **Proverbs 17,18; Psalm 91**

Hebrews 11:8–22

Certainty or Faith

Lord, give us the grace to trust you when we are called to enter an uncertain future.

When I hear people looking for clear guidance I always think of verse 8: 'By faith Abraham, when called to go to a place he would later receive as his inheritance, obeyed and went, even though he did not know where he was going.' As I have thought of this verse over the years, I have concluded that, like Abraham, I would prefer God's gift of faith to any certainty I might have as to what my next steps into the future might look like.

Today we consider the faith of Abraham and Sarah, and the patriarchs Isaac, Jacob and Joseph. When God called Abraham, he went – not knowing where he was going. Abraham, Isaac and Jacob camped in what was later to be the Promised Land. They were like aliens, with their eyes on God's promised future: a city with foundations that went deeper and were more stable than tent pegs, the city that was designed and built by God. This was a future homeland (not the one they had left), a heavenly country, the city God had prepared for them. As for Sarah, even though she was past child-bearing age, by faith she was able to bear the children God had promised. And Joseph? He was so certain that God's promises go beyond the grave that he would not permit his descendants to bury his bones in Egypt.

Notice how everything is oriented towards their future with the God who has promised that he will ultimately dwell with his people.[1] They had assurance about the things they hoped for and the things they could not see, because they knew God and knew God's promise to bless. Thus, they could enter a future that was unclear, but assured, for God was with them.

God promises not certainty, but faith. Ask for faith as you step into the future with assurance that, however the details unfold, God will be with you in them.

[1] Rev 21:3

BIBLE IN A YEAR: **Proverbs 19,20; 1 Thessalonians 2**

Pleasure, or Disgrace?

Lord, grant me the grace to identify with Jesus and his sufferings, whatever the cost.

Today's reading considers events around the Exodus and the conquest of Canaan. Two things seemed to be in the writer's mind. He had already said that the wilderness generation was faithless and that Joshua did not give the people rest.[1] Consequently, he now ignores the wilderness wanderings, jumping from the Exodus to Jericho – and chooses to highlight Rahab over Joshua.

He deals with the faith of Moses' parents and of Moses himself, who rejected association with Pharaoh's court with all its pleasures, choosing instead mistreatment with God's people and 'disgrace for the sake of Christ' (v 26). By faith, Moses also left Egypt unafraid of the Pharaoh's anger and he kept the Passover. Then, by faith, the people went through the Red Sea on dry land. The writer recalls how the walls of Jericho fell by faith (without saying that Joshua initiated this) and how Rahab saved her life when she received the spies in peace. The ultimate outcome of this faithful act is her inclusion in the genealogy of Jesus.[2]

Today's highlight for me is the faith of Moses, who 'regarded disgrace for the sake of Christ as of greater value than the treasures of Egypt, because he was looking ahead to his reward' (v 26). That he identified with Jesus and chose disgrace for his sake sounds incongruous, given that Moses lived hundreds of years before Jesus but, as Harold Attridge suggests, as a prophet 'Moses could have been understood to be aware of the … one who would bring God's promises to reality'.[3] With prophetic insight, Moses saw Jesus, 'the pioneer and perfecter of faith'[4] and chose to identify with him, whatever the cost. In 13:13 the writer will also call us to be prepared to bear the reproach of Christ.

Pray today for those called to suffer for Jesus. Ask God to hear their cries, to strengthen their faith and to give them wisdom and boldness in their witness.

---

[1] Heb 3,4 [2] Matt 1:5 [3] Harold Attridge, *The Epistle to the Hebrews*, Fortress, 1999, p341; for Moses as a prophet see Deut 18:15–18 [4] Heb 12:2

BIBLE IN A YEAR: **Proverbs 21,22; 1 Thessalonians 3**

Heroes of Faith

Lord, strengthen my faith, enabling me to persevere like those I read about today, so that I too can be commended for it.

The question at the start of verse 32 and its reply indicate that the writer reached the climax of his list with Rahab: 'And what more shall I say? I do not have time to tell ...'. He names six individuals plus 'the prophets', followed by nine examples of the great deeds these accomplished though faith. After this the tone changes. While some women received back their dead who were raised to life, there were others who endured various kinds of torture and sometimes martyrdom, suffering extreme cruelty from their persecutors. Those who lived were mistreated horribly and excluded from society, being forced to wander in deserts and mountains and to live in caves and holes in the ground.

The whole catalogue of heroes of faith and their deeds shows how God's faithful people, that great 'cloud of witnesses',[1] have endured by keeping their eyes on the goal while suffering persecution. The implication is that the first readers of Hebrews, who had suffered persecution in the past and were likely to face further persecution in the future, would be encouraged in their faith and motivated to persevere, even if it cost them their lives.[2]

The chapter closes as it began, with the reminder that all these 'ancients' were commended for their faith (see v 2). Nevertheless, none of them received what was promised. For that, they had to wait (v 40). Those of us who follow Christ now and the faithful ones who preceded him are together made perfect through the self-offering of Christ. We, with them, will make up that great company of 'the righteous made perfect'.[3] Together, we will surround the throne in the world to come, where Jesus is now exalted – so long as we endure.

Many believers today are suffering for the name of Jesus. Ask God to strengthen their faith, to hear their cries and to grant them boldness and wisdom in their witness.

[1] Heb 12:1 [2] See Heb 10:32–36; 12:1–4 [3] Heb 12:23

BIBLE IN A YEAR: **Proverbs 23,24; Psalms 92,93**

We Have Sinned. Save Us!

'Praise be to the Lord, the God of Israel, from everlasting to everlasting. Let all the people say, "Amen!"'[1]

The bulk of this psalm recounts the rebellion of God's people in Egypt (v 7), in the desert (vs 13–33), in the Promised Land (vs 34–43) and in the Exile. It is from Exile that they call, 'Save us, LORD our God, and gather us from the nations' (v 47). It is a long story of repeated rebellion, as the lines beginning with 'They' indicate. There are also lines beginning with 'He' – God. In this psalm, God's love and mercy do not come to the fore: the focus is on God's discipline for their faithlessness.

More remarkable, then, are the verses surrounding this litany of rebellion. The psalm begins and ends with a call to praise the Lord.[2] Verses 1–3 celebrate God's goodness, love and mighty acts, and pronounce a blessing on those who do what is right. Verses 4 and 5 are a personal appeal to God to save the psalmist and verse 6 is a communal confession of sin. All this contrasts with the people's rebellion and God's discipline throughout their history.

It is not until we reach the end that we see why the psalmist can be so confident in these opening verses. In verse 44 we find that God took note of their distress, and in verse 45 that 'he remembered his covenant and out of his great love he relented'. In the Bible, when God remembers he acts. This is particularly so when he remembers his covenant. God had made a solemn commitment to be their God and they had committed to be God's people. Despite their ongoing rebellion, God was committed to them. Therefore, they confidently pray, 'Save us LORD our God … that we may give thanks to your holy name and glory in your praise' (v 47).

The appeal in verse 47 is to enable them to give thanks to God. Either alone or with others, remember that God also saved you for this and respond accordingly.

---

[1] Ps 106:48 [2] Technically, verse 48 is a conclusion to the Fourth Book of Psalms (Pss 90–106), but it is also a conclusion to this psalm

BIBLE IN A YEAR: **Proverbs 25,26; 1 Thessalonians 4**

With Eyes Fixed on Jesus

Lord, as much as it is in our power, help us to make the way level and smooth for others in our communities.

Verses 1–3 complete the list of faithful examples by referring to Jesus, 'the pioneer and perfecter of faith' (v 2). Our life is pictured as a race, probably a marathon rather than a sprint, and while some suggest that this cloud of witnesses is watching from the grandstand, I don't think this is the whole picture. In the Bible, a witness is someone with a story to tell. The witnesses are the people of chapter 11 who have testified with their faithful living. While we consider their faith, we are to fix our eyes on Jesus, who endured the shameful death of crucifixion and is now enthroned at God's right hand. When we consider the opposition he endured, it will strengthen us so that we neither grow weary nor lose heart.

Our struggle against sin includes the sin in the lives of the opponents we face, including 'all that motivates and empowers them to persecute believers in the hope of eliciting compromise'.[2] The antidote to growing weary and losing heart is to see it as God's discipline, even though it comes to us from sinners like those Jesus faced.

The idea that these struggles are God's discipline comes from Proverbs 3:11 and 12, words that the Father gives to his children to encourage them. Discipline like this is unlikely to be pleasant, but will have a good outcome, 'a harvest of righteousness and peace' (v 11). Therefore, we are to strengthen our arms and knees and, as we have noticed elsewhere in Hebrews, we are to care for others, ensuring that the paths of any lame members of the community are level and smooth, so that they are not disabled, but healed (v 13).

Do you know of any troubled people whom you can encourage and whose paths you can smooth today? Lift them in prayer and then find a way to help them.

[1] Mark 9:24 [2] Gareth Lee Cockerill, *The Epistle to the Hebrews*, Eerdmans, 2012, p619

BIBLE IN A YEAR: **Proverbs 27,28; 1 Thessalonians 5**

Our Arrival at Mount Zion

Lord, give me ears to hear you speaking, an understanding mind, a receptive heart, and hands and feet ready to do your will.

These verses contain the final warning passage in Hebrews, with a series of commands, some beginning with 'See to it …' (vs 15,16,25). The verses expand on one of the warnings with the only negative example of a named individual in the book, Esau. In contrast to the future orientation of the faithful people in chapter 11, Esau preferred present gratification to future blessing – and was rejected. The warnings get stronger as the chapter proceeds, until we are warned not to refuse 'him who speaks' (v 25). There is no escape for those who turn away from God, when he shakes both earth and heaven to remove what is displeasing to him so that what pleases him remains. The chapter ends with a call to worship with reverence and awe, for 'our "God is a consuming fire"' (v 29).

Embedded here is what Barnabas Lindars calls 'the grand finale of Hebrews',[1] two finely balanced paragraphs about two mountains. The first is plainly Sinai, to which they have not come; the second is Zion, to which they have come. However, this is not the earthly Zion but the heavenly Jerusalem, the city of the living God that Abraham and the patriarchs eagerly anticipated.[2] Jesus is there, and we his followers have access to his presence – even though we are still on earth.

The paragraph about Sinai breathes an atmosphere of darkness and gloom, terror and trembling. The paragraph about Zion exudes light and gladness. Here we encounter angels in joyful worship with all God's people, both living and dead. We have this joyful experience now when we gather to worship with God's people. When we finally reach that 'kingdom that cannot be shaken' (v 28), we will experience this same reality, but in an even fuller measure.

Think of your church, whether large or small, gathering with all God's people, past and present, and myriad angels joyfully worshipping. Does this change your perception of your fellowship?

[1] Barnabas Lindars, 'The Rhetorical Structure of Hebrews', *New Testament Studies* 35, 1989, p402
[2] Heb 11:10

BIBLE IN A YEAR: **Proverbs 29,30; 2 Thessalonians 1**

Hebrews 13:1–16

We have an Altar

Lord, may the words of my lips be pleasing to you as I confess the name of Jesus today.

Hebrews 13 begins with several commands about the behaviour of the readers as a community of God's people. They are to love one another, show hospitality to strangers, remember prisoners, maintain sexual purity and avoid the love of money, remaining content with what they have. They are to remember their former leaders, imitate their faith and consider the outcome of their way of life. Unlike these historical figures, who have died, the Jesus they knew in the past remains the same now and for ever. None of these things have lost their relevance for God's people, even in the twenty-first century.

Then, in a book where the Father, Jesus and the Holy Spirit have spoken the Scriptures to one another and to the community, in verse 6 the community responds by speaking the Scriptures themselves. They affirm that they are not afraid and they ask what mere mortals can do to them with the Lord as their helper. This is a statement of confidence in the God who has resolved to remain with them (v 5).

Finally, the author reverts to 'we' language (vs 6,10,14). We have an altar, he says, probably meaning the sacrifice of Jesus. It was a sacrifice like that offered on the Day of Atonement, where, rather than being eaten by the priests, the animals carcasses were burned outside the camp,[1] prefiguring Jesus's execution outside Jerusalem. This has consequences for the believers. By using 'let us' language (vs 13,15), he encourages them to leave the confines of the city, no longer holy since it was where Jesus was rejected, and go to a formerly unholy place 'outside the camp' (v 13), now holy because Jesus is there. There they bear his disgrace and offer words of praise. There are other sacrifices to offer – doing good and sharing with others, for this is pleasing to God.

These verses contain seven commands. Find them all and examine your life before God to see if you have been neglecting any of them.

---

[1] Lev 16:27

Grace be with You All

Lord Jesus Christ, to whom be glory for ever and ever, I ascribe glory and honour to you today.

These verses give some tantalising hints about the background of Hebrews. 'Pray for us … so that I may be restored to you soon' (vs 18,19) may imply that more than one person was behind Hebrews; that they were absent but one of them hoped to join them soon. Who they were 'only God knows', said the church father Origen.[1] Writer and readers were acquainted with Timothy (v 23) and had a connection with some who were from Italy (v 24), although we don't know whether they were there at the time.

Two other things stand out. First, Hebrews is a 'word of exhortation' (v 22), and we have seen that exhortation and encouragement are important. Here the writer encourages them to have confidence in their leaders and submit to their authority, so that their work will be a joy rather than a burden. The words 'to their authority' (v 17) are absent from the Greek text, and the word for 'submit' only appears here in the Bible. I think *The Message* conveys the idea well, with 'Listen to their counsel'. We are called to listen carefully to those God has placed as leaders in his church. The verse says something about the way leaders lead as well as about how we follow.

Second, note the beautiful benediction in verses 20 and 21, where the writer prays for his people. The resurrection of Jesus is implied by the references to his exaltation to God's right hand (so important in Hebrews), but it is specifically mentioned only here. He asks God, who brought Jesus back from the dead, to equip them with everything good, enabling them to do God's will and live lives pleasing to God. If God raised Jesus from the dead, he can surely equip us to live for him.

Personalise the prayer in verses 20 and 21, asking God to enable you to live a life pleasing to him in every way. And may grace be with you all.

---

[1] Origen speculated they might have been Paul (whose thought was behind Hebrews) and Luke (who did the actual writing)

BIBLE IN A YEAR: **Ecclesiastes 1–3; 2 Thessalonians 2**

HOW TO READ THE BOOK OF ACTS

Reading Acts as Story and Stories

The book of Acts is long! It begins in Jerusalem with a small group of Jesus' followers – some a hundred and twenty (1:15) – who are all Jewish, and this group's initial growth is entirely among Jewish people. The book ends in Rome with a worldwide mission in process, embracing non-Jewish people (Gentiles). How does Luke get from Jerusalem to Rome, from a Jewish sect to a worldwide community? Reading Acts is following this pair of journeys and recognising the big story.

Understanding that *God, now known in Jesus and by the Holy Spirit, is the key actor* in what happens is central. Acts begins by summarising Luke's volume one, his Gospel: 'In my former book, Theophilus, I wrote about all that Jesus began to do and to teach' (1:1). The crucial word is 'began', for Acts tells what Jesus *goes on* to do and teach. Jesus' actions now are different, because he acts from heaven rather than living on earth. Jesus is at the Father's right side (2:33) and the Holy Spirit proceeds from the Father and the Son to empower his people to live and witness for him (1:8). This is a stunning development, for Jewish people understood that God, and God

alone, could give his Spirit to people – but now *Jesus* does that. This places Jesus in the same category as the Father, worthy of the same worship and honour.

A major way that Jesus works on earth is through the Spirit, who empowers believers to speak boldly about Jesus (4:31) and prevents them going in wrong directions (16:6,7). God works by other means too: Luke writes of 'the Lord' acting by opening Lydia's heart to the gospel in Philippi (16:14) and reassuring Paul that his ministry in Corinth is not in vain (18:9,10). God himself acts, too, by calling people to know him (2:39), by fulfilling Scripture (3:18) and, in the future, by restoring all things (3:21).

Recognising God, Father, Son, and Holy Spirit, as the driver of the narrative of Acts is crucial to reading the book aright. Often, Christians read Acts looking for the contribution of the apostles and the believers. However, these human actions are all responses to God's actions and God's initiative. It is God's guidance and power which move the mission forward, not human planning or strategy. Indeed, at times, the believers are dragged along, kicking and screaming, behind God! The movement to include Gentiles is a prime example: God takes the initiative in Philip's mission among Samaritans (8:4–24), in Philip's meeting the Ethiopian official in the middle of nowhere (8:26–40) and in Peter's encounter with the Roman centurion Cornelius' household (ch 10). Even then, Peter meets scepticism when he returns to Jerusalem (11:1–3) and it is only after he tells the story that the Jerusalem believers recognise, 'even to Gentiles God has granted repentance that leads to life' (11:18, my emphasis).

So, in the big story and in individual stories, look for what God is doing. Ask what Luke is saying about God, God's purposes for the world, and the response God seeks from humanity.

Reading Acts as Luke's volume two

Acts is not a free-standing book, but Luke's volume two. So to read Acts well, read it with Luke's Gospel. Here are three examples of how fruitful that can be.

First, the church's mission among Jews and Gentiles is foreshadowed in Luke's Gospel. As far back as Simeon's song of praise,

Jesus' coming is 'a light for revelation to the Gentiles, and the glory of your people Israel' (Luke 2:32). This phrase echoes 'a light for the Gentiles' in Isaiah 49:6, a verse quoted more fully when Paul speaks in Pisidian Antioch (Acts 13:47) and echoed in 1:8 'to the ends of the earth'. Aged Simeon prophetically sees that the infant Jesus brings God's salvation to both Gentiles and Jews – and thus announces the church's dual mission in Acts.

When Paul goes to a new city, his first port of call is the Jewish synagogue (eg 13:14) to announce that Israel's Messiah has come. When, as regularly happens, the synagogue community divides in its response to the gospel, Paul engages with Gentiles (eg 13:44–46). However, in the next city Paul again goes to the synagogue (14:1), so verses like 13:46 do not mean the end of mission among Jewish people.

Second, the mass of teaching by Jesus about *wealth and poverty* in Luke's Gospel – a particular emphasis of this Gospel – is translated into a lifestyle of sharing in Acts. Jesus teaches about the responsibility of relatively wealthy people to care for those in poverty in his parable of the rich man and Lazarus (Luke 16:19–31), and that is played out in Acts by believers who sell property or possessions to help needy believers (Acts 4:32–37, echoing Deuteronomy 15:4). This sharing does not disappear when the believing communities spread around the Roman world, for the Syrian Antioch church (a mix of Jews and Gentiles, Acts 11:19–21) gives generously to support their (predominantly Jewish) Judean sisters and brothers when Agabus prophesies a famine (11:27–30).

Third, there is *a striking shift from focusing on Jesus' death and its meaning in the Gospel, to proclaiming Jesus' resurrection and rule in Acts*. In the Gospel, Jesus announces his forthcoming death (eg Luke 18:31–33) and Luke tells the story fully (Luke 23). Luke does not repeat in Acts what he has said in his Gospel: the focus of the evangelistic speeches in Acts is on what follows Jesus' death – his resurrection and exaltation. Thus Peter's Pentecost speech mentions Jesus' death rather briefly (2:23) and focuses on Jesus' exaltation to the Father's right side by using Scripture in 2:24–36. Peter quotes Psalms 16:8–11 and 110:1 – a verse Jesus himself expounds earlier in Luke 20:42–44. In pagan Athens,

Paul highlights Jesus' right to judge the world on the grounds that he has been raised from the dead (17:30,31; cf 17:18).

These are examples of *seeking patterns in Luke's two books*, for Luke regularly introduces an idea briefly, and then paints it narratively in what follows. It is worth looking at stories of people becoming believers in Acts in relation to the features of conversion in 2:38,39 (repentance, baptism, forgiveness, the gift of the Spirit, joining the believing community). Or consider vignettes of church life throughout Acts as examples of the features of the earliest community in 2:42 (the apostles' teaching, fellowship, meals, prayers).

Reading Acts as history and teaching

Acts is also rooted in *the Greek and Roman world of the first century*. We visit places we know from ancient history, both from writings and archaeological findings. In Athens, on Paul's three-mile walk from the harbour to the centre, he would have encountered dozens of statues and temples to gods and to past Roman emperors worshipped as gods. The city was certainly a forest of idols (17:16) and we know many from the Athenian stone remains and ancient writings. We also know the Epicurean and Stoic philosophers whom Paul encounters (17:18) from their writings and busts of key philosophers. Mars Hill, where the Areopagus (Athens' city council) met, still sits below the Parthenon in Athens (17:19). Luke portrays this world accurately, for example in the naming of local officials in different places: Cyprus has a proconsul resident at Paphos (13:6,7), 'most excellent' is the right way to address a Roman official of equestrian rank (24:3) and Malta has a 'chief official', literally a 'first man' in Greek (28:7). It is worth exploring these connections – a good commentary helps – to see how the gospel message is contextualised in a variety of settings.

In what way is Acts there to *teach* its readers how to think, believe and live? How far is it *prescriptive*, and how far is it merely *descriptive*, telling us what happened without necessarily calling readers to do the same? Here is where pattern-seeking helps: if there is a repeated pattern of events or beliefs or ways of thinking, then it is likely that Luke is commending that to his readers. I suggest above that that is true for the elements of conversion, and of church life.

In addition, Luke uses *speeches* to summarise and highlight key themes, notably about Jesus and the way to respond to him. He frequently records a speech set in a particular context and expects us to assume that the believers speak comparably in similar contexts. Peter's speeches in chapters 2 and 3 are examples of speaking in Jerusalem and Judea. Paul's Pisidian Antioch speech (13:16–47) models speaking in a diaspora synagogue, and Luke signals that: 'The same thing occurred in Iconium' (14:1, NRSV). Likewise, Paul's Athens speech gives a picture of how to communicate among pagans (17:16–31). These speeches are not duplicated – Luke has a limited amount of papyrus roll available! – but they offer models of communicating the gospel in different settings.

FOR FURTHER READING

Tom Wright, *Acts for Everyone*, 2 volumes, SPCK, 2008

Beverly R Gaventa, *Acts*, Abingdon New Testament Commentary, Abingdon, 20034

1 Kings 12–22

NO OTHER GODS

Whom do you worship? That's the question at the centre of God's story of these kings. The glory days of David and Solomon are over. David will henceforth be the benchmark (14:8): a man after God's own heart.[1] Solomon, his son, begins well, building the Lord's Temple – but wealth, power, fame (and women) distract him (11:9–13). Judgement and division come among God's people, setting the scene for the coming decades – ending in defeat, destruction by enemies and long-prophesied exile. The timescale of 1 Kings is from around 971 BC, until just after King Ahab's reign over the northern kingdom ends in 853 BC. 2 Kings then takes over the story until Judah's captivity around 587 BC.

These books may seem to have little relevance to our lives today, but this history is written from God's perspective. At its centre – despite power struggles, politics, warfare, murders and suicide – is the leaders' relationship with God – whether or not they walk in his ways. Pernicious idolatry (golden calves, 12:28)

begins as a political convenience, but within King Jeroboam's reign it becomes endemic. Temple worship in Jerusalem is degraded from golden to bronze.[2] The people are encouraged to forget old ways, with new gods to worship. The litany of good and evil kings continues. When Ahab, the most evil of kings, comes to the throne, God intervenes through his prophet Elijah – the 'troubler of Israel' (18:17). He never stops courageously speaking out against idolatry. The cloud of promise on the horizon may only be tiny (18:44), but Elijah stays focused and, for a while, the people turn to God again.

Note that the lives of these leaders influence others. Our own choices about how we live are not just a personal matter. Inevitably, they affect those we live among – possibly for generations to come. How do we influence others? Are we speaking out for God, challenging evil ways with troubling words from him? Is our own worship of God wholehearted?

'Tricia and Emlyn Williams

[1] Acts 13:22 [2] cf 1 Kings 14:26,27

Decisions

'Show me your ways, Lord, teach me your paths.'[1]

Division begins. It wasn't all the fault of new king Rehoboam. Solomon himself had allowed the creeping seeds of idolatry to take root.[2] Now David's kingdom is left in the unsure hands of a younger man. Perhaps overwhelmed by power and status, he makes unwise decisions which will be significant for the kingdom's future.

Right from the start, the presence of a strong rival is evident. Maybe Jeroboam[3] was the more natural leader (vs 1–4), but he wasn't God's choice for Judah.[4] The people's request that the former king's demands on them should be lightened presents an opportunity. A different decision from Rehoboam might have brought a different history for God's people. The wise elders of Solomon's court suggest a soft response, emphasising the role of king as servant (v 7). In contrast, his friends suggest disrespectful dominance (vs 10,11). Perhaps to his credit, Rehoboam pauses for a significant three days (v 12), but his unwise choice to follow old playmates' advice brings results which would mean trouble for centuries ahead. Jeroboam and the Israelites go 'home' (v 16). Foolishly, the proud, power-hungry Rehoboam decides to show who is boss, which ends in tragedy. A not-so-impressive king flees for his life (v 18). Perhaps influenced by others of his generation, Rehoboam then plans an attack on the new regime of Jeroboam (v 21).

Through it all, there is a continuing whisper of God's sovereign power at work (v 15). Solomon had been warned of the result of his heart's turning from God.[5] Now, however, God mercifully restrains Rehoboam from further divisive action (v 24). God's action (or apparent inaction) in our contemporary world may sometimes puzzle us, but this story challenges us to keep God-centred thinking and decisions at the heart of our living.

Pray for our world and its leaders, that choices may be made today in order that God's will might be done, his kingdom come.

[1] Ps 25:4　[2] 1 Kings 11:7,8　[3] 1 Kings 11:28　[4] 1 Kings 11:29–39　[5] 1 Kings 11:9

BIBLE IN A YEAR: **Ecclesiastes 4,5; 2 Thessalonians 3**

1 Kings 12:25 – 13:10

Golden Calves

'You shall have no other gods before me.'[1] Examine your life before God.

Worship of 'golden calves' (v 28) might remind you of another time in the Israelites' history.[2] Here, in a different context, another leader was trying to avoid trouble – Jeroboam was motivated by political scheming to secure his reign. The issues of idolatry and a new festival (vs 32,33) weren't about God for Jeroboam. They were artifices, to keep the people away from the holy city which might deflect their loyalty. Jeroboam seems to have forgotten Ahijah's prophecy of God's faithfulness to him *if* he stayed true to him.[3]

The promises ('all that your heart desires'[4]) were negated in these days when King Jeroboam's lust for personal power was demonstrated in his blasphemous actions. The rituals at Bethel and the mock priesthood (v 32) were about 'his own choosing' (v 33). So, 'a man of God' (13:1) speaks judgement (v 2).

Jeroboam thinks he can defy God's Word by ordering the man's arrest (v 4), but God will not be silenced – and Jeroboam's attention is caught for a moment in recognition of his shrivelled hand (v 6). His healing prompts an offer of hospitality – but the prophet's response (v 8) suggests that this was not rooted in true repentance or gratitude. Rather, it seems that Jeroboam was still scheming to avoid a possible threat to his image and power. At this point, 'the man of God' is resolute – he obeys God, not man (vs 8–10).

It doesn't seem that Jeroboam was personally feeling an affinity towards other gods. Rather, he was guilty of a kind of idolatry of himself: my kingdom, my power (12:26,27). We might see such destructive characteristics demonstrated in our own world today – but the Word of God here isn't just for powerful rulers; it speaks to the hidden pride of our own hearts.

What are the 'golden calves' in your life? What excuses do you make to yourself and others for their presence? Re-root yourself in God.

[1] Exod 20:3 [2] Exod 32:1–4 [3] 1 Kings 11:37,38 [4] 1 Kings 11:37

BIBLE IN A YEAR: **Ecclesiastes 6,7; Psalms 95,96**

Give Thanks to the Lord

Whatever life is like for you and your family at the moment, pause to give thanks to God whose 'love endures for ever'.[1]

The psalmist leads the congregation in a celebration of their history: these things have happened – disasters, hunger, thirst, illness, exile, imprisonment, rebellion, dangers and trouble (vs 4–32); and God blessed them, rescued them and continues to love them (vs 33–42). Some have thought that this psalm must refer to post-exilic Israel, with its references to gathering (vs 2,3), rescue from captivity (vs 10–16) and the settlement of the land. As we read, however, the stories of multiple individuals come to mind from across the vast landscape of God's people and their experience – and its images bring echoes of our own lives and those we know who also live in God's story. Whatever its precise time, the congregation sang its words from the perspective of knowing their history and celebrating God's redemption. Notice that, at times, these people have got into trouble because of their own foolishness and rebellion; at other times, they suffered because of others' actions or natural events. Yet, whatever the cause, God intervened to save his people when 'they cried to the LORD in their trouble' (vs 13,19,28), because of his 'unfailing love' (v 8). The focus changes in verses 33–42. Away from *our* suffering, the perspective moves to God's intervention and his transformative actions of judgement and blessing – from desert to harvest, from oppression to rejoicing: '*He* turned the desert into pools of water' (see v 35); '*He* blessed them' (see v 38); '*He* lifted the needy' (see v 41).

Throughout the psalm, the rhythm of the repeated lines ('they cried out'; 'he saved them'; 'give thanks') gives us a rhythm for our own lives and worship. We are invited to join in the rejoicing with God's people today. Together, let *us* ponder anew 'the loving deeds of the LORD' (v 43).

'Let the redeemed of the LORD tell their story' (v 2). Who will you tell? Whose story will you learn from and rejoice? How will you 'heed' wisdom (v 43)?

[1] Ps 107:1

BIBLE IN A YEAR: **Ecclesiastes 8,9; 1 Timothy 1**

Listen and Obey

'Blessed ... are those who hear the Word of God and obey it.'[1]

Am I listening to God? Today's verses may seem harsh. There are two men – the 'man of God' from Judah and the 'old prophet' of Bethel (v 11). The first acts obediently, but then seems to lose focus and disobeys God. As a result, he dies violently and alone (v 24). Why so serious a consequence?

The wider context is important. The 'man of God' from Judah had a significant commission. If King Jeroboam of Bethel didn't have a change of heart, disaster and death lay ahead for *all* the people of Israel. He had understood, including the instructions not to linger in a place of compromise (vs 8,9). Then came this incident on his return. What distracted him? The old prophet seemed trustworthy, speaking in ways which suggested common understanding (v 18). In fact, however, he was lying. He *may* have been trying to be kind, but even so,

his words casually present the temptation to disobey God – and it's clear that the 'man of God' knew this (vs 16,17,21,22). Back on the road, he is killed – this 'lion' and 'donkey' of a man – his body left on the road for passers-by to see (vs 24,25). Eventually, the old prophet buries his remains with respect (v 30) – but it's too late (v 32). Why should Jeroboam and his people take notice of the 'man of God' who didn't keep God's command (vs 8,9,17,19,21,26)? The result? Jeroboam didn't change. His sinful activity continued, leading to the downfall of Israel and the house of Jeroboam, and its 'destruction from the face of the earth' (v 34).

Temptation to disobey God's voice comes in subtle ways. On the main stage we're strong; but on the everyday journeys of life we hear soft, surprising voices calling us away from God's path.

What unlikely voices are getting in the way of your hearing and obeying God?

[1] Luke 11:28

BIBLE IN A YEAR: **Ecclesiastes 10,11; 1 Timothy 2**

Walking in Obedience

Thank God for all he has given you. Pray that you will keep your eyes on him alone.

The two, separated kingdoms – despite their 'continual warfare' (v 30) – are now established. Jeroboam, *not* a son of Solomon, is king of Israel; Rehoboam, son of Solomon, grandson of David, is king of Judah. 'If you … walk in obedience to me'[1] is the lynch-pin.

Jeroboam had already failed on his side of the agreement.[2] Today's reading tells of God's judgement. His son had become ill (v 1). The king's wife goes to talk to Ahijah the prophet. He had given good news before[3] – perhaps he would again. But why the disguise? In any case, the prophet was blind! However, the woman couldn't hide from God. The prophet knows who is coming before the knock at his door. He knows what she will ask; and God's answer – 'he will give Israel up because of the sins Jeroboam has committed and has caused' (v 16). The son's death ('the only one … in whom the LORD … has found anything good', v 13) is a preface to the future for Jeroboam's family (vs 8–11).

Rehoboam had sometimes listened to God,[4] but he didn't have the wholeheartedness of his grandfather. It is the people of Judah who are *named* as doing 'evil in the eyes of the LORD' (v 22), but it is the king who allowed his people's 'detestable practices' (v 24). The great treasures of the Temple and palace are taken (vs 25,26) and Rehoboam replaces gold with bronze. After the glory days of King Solomon, Rehoboam's reign signals decline. His story (and Jeroboam's) reminds us that God is concerned not only with our personal attitude towards him, but also with our influence on others. It takes courage to lead in listening to God and to live in obedience to him.

Pray for courage to lead in ways which help others to honour and obey God.

[1] 1 Kings 11:38 [2] 1 Kings 13:34 [3] 1 Kings 11:38 [4] 1 Kings 12:21–24

BIBLE IN A YEAR: **Ecclesiastes 12; 1 Timothy 3**

1 Kings 15:1–32

Bad King, Good King

'God is working his purpose out, as year succeeds to year.'[1]

Now, the writer gets going on the chronicle of kings of Judah and Israel. Snapshots of their reigns interweave, telling parallel stories of God's people. Today, we hear about the contrasting rules of two kings of Judah (Abijah and Asa) and then, Nadab, king of Israel. From our twenty-first-century perspective, such passages might seem far-removed, historical tales. But pause – notice how these accounts are written from *God's* point of view, reflecting on the behaviour of *his* people. How might his prophets write about us today?

For both Abijah and Asa, we are reminded of their special ancestry as descendants of King David, through Maakah (vs 2,10). Abijah's sins and lack of devotion to God do not bring peace to the land (v 6) and his reign is short. Yet, there is forbearance on God's part because of David's faithfulness (v 4) and the special role of Jerusalem (a lamp, v 4).[2] Unlike his father, Asa 'did what was right in the eyes of the LORD' (v 11). Doing 'right' for forty-one years (vs 10,11) could not have been easy! Imagine the opposition he would have encountered in acting to rid God's people of their idolatry, even deposing the Queen Mother (vs 11–13). Despite his faults, his 'heart was fully committed to the LORD' (v 14). The rest of his reign was taken up with proactive work, establishing a prosperous land for God's people (vs 16–22).

Back in the northern kingdom of Israel, the evil influence of King Jeroboam persists (v 26) and God's Word is fulfilled.[3] Nadab, his son, is killed by Baasha, another pretender to the throne, who goes on to kill all of Jeroboam's family (v 29). God is faithful and working his purposes out in mysterious ways.

How do you think God is working out his purposes through your life? Ask God to help you to be persistent and courageous in leadership.

---

[1] Arthur C Ainger, 1841–1919 [2] See also 1 Kings 11:36 [3] 1 Kings 14:14

BIBLE IN A YEAR: **Song of Songs 1,2; Psalms 97,98**

Evil Times

How can we live good lives in times of evil?

Against the backdrop of Asa's reign in Judah, the bad kings of Israel follow one another in quick succession, all doing 'evil in the eyes of the LORD' (16:19,25,30). There is a thread through these verses: they all follow 'the ways of Jeroboam' (16:2,26) in idolatry. Our influence may last long beyond the years of our lives. How are we living and influencing others in our own evil times? We have choices – even when things don't look promising.

Baasha had been raised up and 'appointed' (16:2) ruler by the Lord to end the dynasty of Jeroboam (15:29). Eventually, however, he followed the ways of the old king and, like Ahijah, Jehu prophesies his judgement (16:1–3). The kingdom falls into civil war (and drunken parties among the leadership, v 9). Power struggles, murder and rebellion end Baasha's dynasty (v 12). These accounts are not just about ancient politics. The root cause of these evil times is rulers who put 'worthless' idols (v 26) at the centre of their own lives, causing those they lead to sin against God too.

The assassination of King Elah leads to Zimri's suicide (v 18) and a military coup. Troubled times bring another dynasty to power – Omri is the father of Ahab (v 28). Both continue in the evil ways of Jeroboam. Omri develops Israel's hill city of Samaria (with its enduring significance)[1] and Ahab does more evil than any before him. For him, the sins of Jeroboam were 'trivial' (v 31)! Influenced by his wife, he gives himself to service of Baal and builds a temple to him (vs 31,32). God is angry (v 33) and will bring judgement, but that won't bring easy living for the faithful minority who serve God.[2]

What are the idols in your own life – they might seem 'trivial' – which are weakening your commitment to God and that of others whom you influence?

[1] John 4:20 [2] 1 Kings 19:18

BIBLE IN A YEAR: **Song of Songs 3,4; 1 Timothy 4**

Truth to Power

Pray for the courage to call out wrongdoing, even if it's costly for you.

As if from nowhere, Elijah the prophet appears. Ahab's kingship had marked a new low for Israel,[1] but now Elijah challenges his attempt to establish Baal worship as the state religion of Israel. The Lord, not Baal,[2] is God of Israel (v 1). Baal was the Canaanite storm god, but the Lord is the one in control. There would be no more rain until Elijah spoke.

Not surprisingly, this didn't go down well with King Ahab, but the Lord was in control. Whilst Israel had to endure drought and the accompanying famine, the Lord told Elijah where to hide. The ravine at Kerith was secure, had water and was exactly the kind of place where ravens roost and store surplus food. Elijah was learning that the Lord can be trusted. As we shall soon see, however, he doesn't always deliver in the way we expect.

The brook eventually dries up, but the Lord stays faithful and sends Elijah to Zarephath for food (v 9). Ironically, Zarephath is outside Israelite territory in Phoenicia, the home of the one from whom he is escaping![3] At the town gate, where hospitality was usually dispensed, he meets a widow and asks for a little water and a piece of bread. In a famine this was a big ask – she is right at the end of her resources (v 12). Elijah, however, asks her to go home and make some bread (v 13). God will provide. Remarkably, she does just that and Elijah's promise is fulfilled (v 16). There is one more test for her. Even though God has provided food, her son later dies. Elijah has no explanation, but cries out to the Lord (v 21) – and the Lord responds (vs 22,23).

Centuries later, Jesus commends this woman's faith,[4] even though she was a Phoenician. Are there people who surprise you by their willingness to obey God?

[1] 1 Kings 16:30 [2] 1 Kings 16:31 [3] 1 Kings 18:4; 16:31 [4] Luke 4:24–26

BIBLE IN A YEAR: **Song of Songs 5,6; 1 Timothy 5**

Troubler of Israel

Pray 'for kings and all those in authority, that we may live peaceful and quiet lives in all godliness and holiness.'[1]

Three years into the drought, the situation was desperate. Ahab and Obadiah divided the country between them and walked through the land looking for fodder for their animals (vs 5,6). Now the Lord spoke again, telling Elijah to visit Ahab: he is going to send rain on the land (v 1). Everyone will benefit, good and bad alike![2]

Obadiah was the chief servant in the royal palace, but he was also a devout believer (v 3). When Jezebel was having the Lord's prophets killed, he hid a hundred of them in caves and fed and watered them (v 4). He was just the person who was needed at that time. 'The Lord has his faithful servants planted in the places they are least expected so that they can carry out the work of God where it is most opposed.'[3]

Whilst Obadiah was searching, Elijah met him – no doubt his hairy clothes and leather belt made him easy to recognise[4] – and told him to let Ahab know that he was there (v 8). For Obadiah, that felt like a death sentence (v 9). Seemingly, Elijah had a reputation for being elusive, like The Scarlet Pimpernel, and Obadiah feared that when he told Ahab, Elijah might disappear again, and it would be doom for him (v 12). However, Elijah could be trusted and he confirmed his promise with an oath (v 15). Keeping his word, Elijah told Ahab the unpopular truth about himself and his family and set in motion plans for a huge contest between himself and the prophets of Baal and of Asherah. This 'troubler of Israel' (v 17) was not afraid to speak truth to power.

Are there things you need to say to powerful people – politicians, church leaders, business people, even family members? Ask for courage to speak up clearly.[5]

[1] 1 Tim 2:2 [2] Matt 5:45 [3] Musa Gotom, in *Africa Bible Commentary*, ed by T Adeyemo, Zondervan, 2006, p437 [4] 2 Kings 1:8 [5] Esth 4:14

BIBLE IN A YEAR: **Song of Songs 7,8; Psalms 99–101**

Psalm 108

God-Centred Worship

'Be exalted, O God, above the heavens; let your glory be over all the earth.'[1]

After days of reflecting on the ups and downs of rulers who didn't want God at the centre of their lives, we come to this worship song of King David. Here was someone who followed God with all his heart.[2] What might we (and those other rulers of God's people) learn for our own praise and prayer from these words?

The psalm, drawing on words from Psalms 57 and 60, begins with the writer's intention to praise and exalt God. His words are not just about personal thanksgiving but express the desire that his and the people's worship will testify to God's greatness 'among the nations' (v 3). He wants God's glory and faithfulness to be known all over the earth (v 5). Worship is witness. Having acknowledged who reigns, the psalmist then cries out: 'Save us and help us' (v 6). This isn't a random prayer. It arises from confidence in God's love for them and his faithfulness (vs 4,6). Rehearsing words about God's sovereign control (vs 7–9), King David recalls the special place of Judah and God's disdain of his people's old enemies (Moab, Edom and Philistia). God is victorious.

Like David, we, his people, know this, but... there *are* times when God seems distant and we feel alone.[3] We may wonder if our failures are because God has rejected us and is no longer with us (v 11). How then should we live in desperate times? This leader doesn't turn *from* God because of hard times. Instead he addresses his people's heartfelt needs *to* God (v 11). He is sustained by hope – human endeavour is worthless, but God's faithfulness *will* bring victory (vs 12,13). The prayer's cry for help is embedded in worship to our King.

'Great is thy faithfulness, O God my Father'.[4] Praise God for all he has provided and for all he will provide.

---

[1] Ps 108:5 [2] 1 Kings 14:8 [3] 1 Kings 18:22 [4] Thomas Obadiah Chisholm, 1866–1960

BIBLE IN A YEAR: **Isaiah 1,2; 1 Timothy 6**

A Minority of One

'The dearest idol I have known, / whate'er that idol be, / help me to tear it from thy throne, / and worship only thee.'[1]

King Ahab, along with people from all over Israel and the prophets of Baal and Asherah (vs 19,20) come together at Mount Carmel as Elijah has requested. He poses a simple challenge (v 21), but in the process puts his finger on the key issue, syncretism. They want to hedge their bets and serve both the Lord and Baal. As a weather god, Baal would be particularly useful in a drought – but the Lord will brook no rival.[2] Elijah follows his verbal challenge with a physical contest (v 23). He calls for two bulls to be brought. Baal's prophets can choose one and prepare it for sacrifice. Elijah can prepare the other. Neither can set the sacrifice alight: they must wait to see which god answers by fire (v 24). Simple prayer for rain will prove nothing, but fire will reveal which god has responded.

At this critical time for himself and his people, Elijah weaponises humour. Baal's prophets call on their god for most of the day (v 29). When they ask him to answer them, nothing happens. They shout, they dance – still nothing happens. Elijah starts to tease them. 'Shout louder!' he says, giving some helpful (!) suggestions as to why he's not answering (vs 27,28). It's not unlike the ridiculous reasons Jesus suggested for people not going to the great banquet in his parable.[3]

In contrast, when it's finally Elijah's turn to ask for fire (v 30), he repairs the altar for the sacrifice. He makes things as difficult as possible for his God, drenching everything in water (vs 33,34). And then he prays. Now we discover his real agenda (vs 36,37). Water is not the issue, faithful trust in God is. And so lightning brings fire from a cloudless sky, precursor to torrential rain (v 45)!

Ask God to pinpoint areas of your life where you are trying to have it both ways, serving two masters.[4]

---

[1] William Cowper, 1731–1800, 'Oh! For a closer walk with God' [2] Exod 20:3 [3] Luke 14:15–24 [4] Matt 6:24

BIBLE IN A YEAR: **Isaiah 3–5; 2 Timothy 1**

A Gentle Whisper

'Speak through the earthquake, wind, and fire, / O still, small voice of calm!'[1]

Emotional highs are often followed by emotional lows – and we crash. Has that happened to you? Here, Elijah's life is under genuine threat (v 2). The courage he'd shown at Carmel has evaporated in the desert heat and he runs away (v 3). So many times I've echoed his words, 'I have had enough, LORD' (v 4)! He lies down under the only shade available in the desert and goes to sleep. An angel wakes him and gives him fresh bread and water – twice (vs 5,7)! – and he makes his escape to Horeb (v 8). He may have felt that he needed a dramatic solution to his problems, but simple food, drink and sleep did the trick (as they often do).

God speaks to Elijah again, asking what he is doing there (v 9b), only for him to pour out his self-pity (v 10). Has he learnt nothing from Mount Carmel? Is God a local god who can only speak at Horeb (Sinai)? Is Elijah really alone?[2] God's answer is simple, just as it was when he provided for him in the desert (v 6). It's not in powerful winds, earthquake or fire, it comes in a gentle whisper, 'a brief sound of silence'.[3] Whether or not we're aware of it, God is at work. Elijah receives new orders (vs 15–17). Hazael, Jehu and Elisha will play significant parts in God's purposes for the future.[4]

With twelve pairs of oxen (v 19), Elisha must have had quite a large farm with at least enough labourers to drive the other eleven pairs. Receiving Elijah's cloak was the equivalent of being anointed: the blessing was passed on to him. Just as, much later, Jesus' disciples would leave their nets,[5] Elisha slaughtered his oxen and burnt his farming equipment. There was to be no turning back from this call.

What has it meant to you to follow Jesus' call? Is anything getting in the way of full obedience?

[1] JG Whittier, 'Dear Lord and Father of Mankind' [2] 1 Kings 18:4 [3] *New Bible Commentary*, IVP, p360
[4] 2 Kings 2; 8; 9 [5] Mark 1:16–18

BIBLE IN A YEAR: **Isaiah 6,7; 2 Timothy 2**

Whose War?

'For our struggle is not against flesh and blood, but ... against the powers of this dark world and against the spiritual forces of evil in the heavenly realms.'[1]

Where is God in this situation? We need to stay aware of the big story of God's purposes. We won't find all the answers, but look out for clues and God-perspectives. Having seen the behaviour of Israel's kings, especially Ahab's, God's intervention on his people's behalf may seem surprising, but it wasn't time for the northern kingdom to fall yet. Samaria (Ahab's capital) is threatened by enemies from Aram, led by Ben-Hadad (probably Ben-Hadad II). A war of words ensues (vs 1–12). It's hard to distinguish at first between arrogant posturing, sarcastic words and serious intent: 'Yes, you can have all my wives (the best ones) and wealth!' (see vs 3,4). Then it dawns on Ahab, 'this man is looking for trouble'! Ben-Hadad's serious (even if drunken, v 12) threats prompt a provocative 'Don't count your chickens' response (v 11). At this point, God intervenes (vs 13,14). Despite Ahab's evil activities, God sometimes speaks directly to him, pursuing his recognition ('then you will know ...' v 13). For a moment, Ahab expresses his need of God's direction and readiness to obey (v 14).

Of course, Ben-Hadad's vast army are not simply engaging in a sport of kings, they are challenging God and his people. The Lord, speaking through his prophet, leads the way (vs 13,14). Humanly, the odds were in the Aramaeans' favour. In God's story, Israel's soldiers were relatively few; the individuals chosen to fight were low-ranking provincials (v 19). Assumptions on Ben-Hadad's part (v 18) perhaps betray a proud presumption of victory and preparation for peace, but there will be no mercy on Israel's side (vs 18–21)! The Aramaean forces are decimated and their king, Ben-Hadad, flees (v 20). God is on his people's side. Get ready for the next battle (v 22)!

What battles are you fighting at the moment? Where is God in this? Be quiet for a few moments, asking him to show you his way ahead.

---

[1] Eph 6:12

What the Lord Says

'This is the way; walk in it.'[1] Which way is the Lord asking you to walk in today?

Who is in charge here? At first it might seem just another episode of war between ancient kings and forgotten kingdoms. The spring season brings another battle between Ben-Hadad and Ahab (v 26); the first knows nothing of God, the other ignores him. But look again. There is another presence (vs 22,28,42) – it is the Lord who wages war for his people and their future.

With their false understandings of gods, the Aramaeans decide their troops will do better if they fight 'on the plains' (v 23). They do not know the God of Israel! Imagine a drone perspective of the vast army of the Aramaeans stretching out over the landscape lined up against the Israelites. Opposite are two small camps looking 'like two small flocks of goats' (v 27). Humanly speaking, the outcome seems obvious, but the enemy, as God had said, is defeated (v 28). Again, the Aramaean king flees (vs 30,20). To complete the job, Ahab needs to be strong and to exercise God's judgement. Instead, appeals (v 32) from the enemy and compromise ('an old ally', v 32) result in the enemy's freedom and return to the status quo (vs 33,34). God is not happy with Ahab or his easiest-way-out strategy. He speaks again through his prophet.

The lived-out story in verses 35–43 may at first seem difficult to understand. Remember, this is not a separate biblical tale, but the closing reflection on an enemy's threat to destroy God's people. Ahab, with God's help, was commissioned and equipped to destroy this threat (vs 13,28) – but he had chosen compromise (v 34). The prophet tells a sulky Ahab of God's judgement on his failure (vs 42,43). As with Jeroboam, it wasn't just the personal consequences that mattered, but those of all God's people.

Sometimes, compromise might seem the easiest (the politest, kindest, best for our image) solution. Ask God for strength and courage to hear and obey his Word.

[1] Isa 30:21

BIBLE IN A YEAR: **Isaiah 10–12; 2 Timothy 3**

No Deal!

'... after desire has conceived, it gives birth to sin; and sin, when it is full-grown, gives birth to death.'[1]

It was a reasonable enough enquiry. The vineyard of Ahab's neighbour would make a convenient vegetable plot for the palace – Naboth might be happy to sell it to him. There are issues to resolve, however. Ahab would have been aware of the sacredness of land as inheritance (v 3). Naboth's response is perfectly understandable. More than that – Ahab, from his position of power, was inviting Naboth to act against God's words to his people.

A grumpy Ahab, seemingly overreacting to the no-deal response, is chided by his proud, scheming, idolatrous wife from Phoenicia.[2] As a Baal-worshipper, she didn't know or care about God's laws and land. She is motivated by getting what *she* wants, deluded by the power of status (v 7). She lays an elaborate and deceitful plot (breaking four of God's Ten Commandments) – arising from the unlawful coveting of another's possessions (vs 8–14) – to commit murder and steal Naboth's vineyard (v 16). The main player in the story is Jezebel, but notice that it all happens on Ahab's authority, the result of his pride (v 8). Their petty self-indulgence and disrespect of others arises from lack of respect for God (v 7). He is on the side of the faithful poor – their lives and well-being matter to him (remember, Nathan's lamb).[3]

Ahab doesn't learn. This time, Elijah brings the Lord's words of judgement (vs 17–24). The king didn't pause to reflect (or wait for probate) and Elijah finds him in Naboth's vineyard (vs 18,19). As with Jeroboam, disaster lies ahead for Ahab's dynasty. Again, it's not just because of his *own* sin, but because of his influence on the people of Israel (v 22). For a while, Ahab appears repentant and God is ready to be merciful (vs 27–29). It won't last...

What might it mean for you to love God and your neighbour as yourself, with no compromise?[4]

[1] James 1:15 [2] 1 Kings 16:31 [3] 2 Sam 12:1–6 [4] Matt 22:37–40

BIBLE IN A YEAR: **Isaiah 13,14; 2 Timothy 4**

1 Kings 22:1–28

First Seek the Lord

'... seek first his kingdom and his righteousness'.[1]

Wars and rumours of wars abounded in the time of the kings of Israel and Judah, but for a short time there was peace between Aram (Syria) and Israel (v 1). The lull seems to have given Ahab time to recover from a brief spell of meekness.[2] A visit from Judah's King Jehoshaphat (King Asa's son) prompts an unusual alliance between the two. It's convenient, maybe, for the scheming, power-hunting Ahab – a possible way to strengthen forces for his Ramoth Gilead venture and to score points for his own prowess (vs 3,4). King Ben-Hadad's earlier offer to return the captured cities[3] seems to have been forgotten. However, Jehoshaphat brings a word of wisdom, challenging the king's yes-men: 'First seek the counsel of the LORD' (vs 4,5,7).

As with situations in our world today, the ruler, without understanding, makes a gesture to silence those who raise inconvenient questions (vs 5,7) – Ahab *needs* Judah's resources (v 4). He grudgingly agrees to ask the one remaining prophet of the Lord for insight (v 8). At first, Micaiah goes along with the king's supporters. Then, critically, Ahab asks the prophet to tell him the truth in the Lord's name (v 16). Imagine the courage Micaiah will have needed, standing alone, amid the sycophantic voices who only seek to curry favour with a king who rejects God's rule. The prophet's word for Ahab is not what he wanted (v 23). The result isn't easy for Micaiah either. The king discounts his words from the Lord with an 'I told you so' (see v 18). A so-called 'prophet' contemptuously slaps him in the face, casting doubt on his words (v 24). Faithful Micaiah is thrown into prison – he leaves, urging the people to remember God's Word (v 28).

Ask the Lord to give you courage to speak the truth in his name – even when the cost to you personally is high.

---

[1] Matt 6:33 [2] 1 Kings 21:27 [3] 1 Kings 20:34

BIBLE IN A YEAR: **Isaiah 15,16; Psalm 103**

God of the Poor

'He stands at the right hand of the needy.'[1]

Here is a prayer for those who feel alone in their commitment to God. It is written by David – this 'man of prayer' (v 4). He is persecuted, hated undeservedly, undermined by lies (vs 2–5). He is hurt (v 22). He is ill (v 24). He is the laughing-stock of his mockers (v 25). Perhaps, in our own ministries and lives, we have felt ourselves to be in a similar place, but, like David (and like Elijah[2]), we turn to our faithful God, trusting in his love for us (v 26).

As twenty-first-century Christians, we may feel uncomfortable with appeals for God's judgement (vs 6–15), but perhaps we have not experienced directly the cruelty of evil leaders who do not respect God's ways. As I write, Christian friends in Ukraine are crying out to God for his judgement on evil. David's prayer is not just a tit-for-tat diatribe. God is sovereign. The judgements David prays for are the reversal of his oppressors' own actions (vs 16–20). In a sense, these are the result of their own godless behaviour (remember Jeroboam[3]). In his desperation, David knows that *he* is powerless, at the end of his own strength (vs 21–25). He can only throw himself on God's love, *for* God's sake (v 21).

When we're desperate, here are lessons for our own prayers. Consistently, we are to acknowledge our sovereign God and his faithfulness (vs 1,21,26). Persistently, we are to look for *his* solutions and activity, rather than trying to fix things ourselves. With determination, we are to keep praising and extolling our God (v 30). And always, we must remember that God stands with those who know that they are 'poor and needy' (vs 22,31).

Like the psalmist, we live in chaotic times. Bring your particular concerns to God now. Ask him to help you stand with those who are poor and in need.

[1] Ps 109:31 [2] 1 Kings 19:9,10 [3] 1 Kings 13:33,34

BIBLE IN A YEAR: **Isaiah 17–20; Titus 1**

1 Kings 22:29–53

Whom will you Serve?

**'... who ... made himself nothing by taking the very nature of a servant ...
Therefore God exalted him ... that at the name of Jesus every knee should bow'.[1]**

Lies might get the popular vote, but God is not deceived. Hedging his bets, Ahab goes to the battle in disguise (v 30), while generously (?) encouraging Jehoshaphat to mark himself out in his royal robes. Ben-Hadad, however, only wants to kill the double-crossing Ahab (vs 31–33). Duplicitous (and cowardly?) Ahab is wounded by a random shot (v 34). Despite his request to be taken out of the battle, he is left facing the enemy. As God had told him, he would die – and the blood of this king who had prostituted himself in idol worship is licked up by dogs (vs 37,38). A shameful end for this shameful king.

Jehoshaphat meanwhile has a long reign and follows the example of his father King Asa. Apart from some exceptions, he also does what 'was right in the eyes of the LORD' (v 43) – though there is some wavering with a failed gold-hunting expedition (v 48). He is still in touch with the powerful northern dynasty, but at least he refuses the temptation to cooperate again with his idolatrous neighbours (vs 49,53).

This first book of Kings ends with the unresolved issues of earlier decades. Judah and Israel are divided. The gentler kings of Judah do 'what was right' (v 43), yet never quite separate themselves or their people from cultural expressions of dependency on other gods ('high places', v 43). In the northern kingdom of Israel, life continues in the ways of ancestor Jeroboam (v 53). Ahaziah, son of Ahab and successor to the throne of Jeroboam, follows the example of his elders, leading the people into sin (v 52). The influence of these leaders over the years has sown the seeds of coming disaster. Their lives bring us back to the question of our own wholehearted devotion to God.

Whom do you serve? Total commitment to God and his ways? Or is there closet dependence on unseen idols out on the hills?

[1] Phil 2:6–10

BIBLE IN A YEAR: **Isaiah 21,22; Titus 2**

"I DON'T GO TO CHURCH BUT..."

95% of under-18s don't go to church. **BUT** many are open to faith.

Together we can reach them!

SCAN TO JOIN **THE 95 CAMPAIGN** FOR FREE

FIND OUT MORE AT THE95.ORG.UK

Mark 1–4

HOPE AMID SUFFERING

Mark's Gospel is held by most scholars to be the first Gospel written. It does not name its author, but tradition ascribes it to John Mark.[1] John Mark was a companion of the apostles Paul and Peter, and his mother's house in Jerusalem was a gathering place for the first Christians.[2]

Our study is on the first four chapters of Mark's Gospel. These verses encourage us to draw conclusions about Jesus' identity from the authority he demonstrates: the authority shown in his teaching, his forgiveness of sins and his power over evil spirits and nature. Mark sets out compelling evidence for Jesus' being the long-awaited Messiah. However, he also makes it clear that, despite this evidence, many people opposed Jesus from the beginning. Hence, Jesus' death on the cross is shown as an inevitable part of a ministry which divided people from the start, rather than something that could have been avoided. It was important to show Jesus' suffering as part of God's plan, for many of Mark's contemporaries would have questioned whether someone who had been executed as a criminal could really be the Messiah. After all, the common expectation was that the Christ would defeat Israel's Roman oppressors, not be killed by them. Early Christians who faced persecution for their faith must also have had questions: if Jesus came to bring in God's kingdom, as he taught, why were they still suffering at the hands of evil?[3] Mark's message is that Christ's suffering does not disprove that Jesus is the Messiah, for the cross was central to his ministry.

This is an important message for us, too, in our in-between times. Although Jesus' ministry has given us a taste of God's kingdom, his kingdom is yet to come fully, which means that evil persists. As we navigate this fallen world, Mark's Gospel reminds us of the victory Jesus won through his suffering and it encourages us that, even though we may face opposition, nothing can stop the progress of God's kingdom.

Caroline Fletcher

---

[1] Eusebius, *Hist. Eccl.* 3.39.15 [2] Acts 12:12 [3] See further, JB Green et al (eds), *Dictionary of Jesus and the Gospels*, IVP, 1992, p524–5

Trusting in the Silence

'But do not forget this one thing, dear friends: with the Lord a day is like a thousand years, and a thousand years are like a day.'[1]

Four hundred years had passed between the latest writings of our Old Testament and these events in Mark's Gospel. The Jewish nation had been without a prophet all that time, and life had been tough. They had been oppressed by the Greeks and were dominated by the Romans. This period is referred to as the silent years, because God did not seem to be speaking to his people any more.[2]

Mark's Gospel dramatically breaks that silence, revealing that the plans God set in place centuries before had not been forgotten but were coming to fruition. Mark does this by emphasising the link between John the Baptist and the prophets of old. He describes John as the forerunner to the Messiah, the one who fulfils prophecies found in Isaiah and Malachi.[3] His description of John also reminds us of the prophet Elijah, with his ascetic clothing and wilderness home, and Elijah was expected to return to usher in the Messiah.[4]

It's easy to see why this time in history was an ideal one for Jesus and John to be active. After such a long period without a prophet, the people were receptive. We read that the 'whole Judean countryside and all the people of Jerusalem' rushed to see the Baptist (v 5), whereas in the past prophets had been mocked and rejected. Secular events helped too, such as the conquests of Alexander the Great which led to Greek becoming a universal language. This would help the gospel to spread around the world, as would the extensive Roman road system.

When God appears to be inactive and we are suffering, it can be hard to keep on trusting. However, today's reading is a reminder that God never forgets us. The Lord's plans and timing are perfect.

'Now faith is being sure of what we hope for and certain of what we do not see.'[4] Reflect on this verse.

---

[1] 2 Pet 3:8 [2] Except in the deuterocanonical books [3] Isa 40:3; Mal 3:1
[4] 2 Kings 1:8; 1 Kings 19:1–15, Mal 4:5 [5] Heb 11:1

BIBLE IN A YEAR: **Isaiah 23,24; Titus 3**

Mark 1:9–20

Thrown in at the Deep End!

Reflect on how you have grown in your faith over time. What events, people and experiences were central to this growth? Spend time giving thanks for them.

When someone begins a new job, they are usually given time to settle in, receiving training before beginning the new role in earnest. John's baptism marks the start of Jesus' ministry. However, Jesus didn't get a gentle introduction. Mark uses his favourite word, 'immediately', to indicate that the wilderness experience quickly followed on from the Lord's baptism (v 12, AV). Jesus' encounter with Satan was no unfortunate accident: Mark stresses that this was the work of the Holy Spirit. He says the Spirit 'sent' Jesus out into the wilderness. There is no doubt that this was God's will.

However, Satan was not the only threat Jesus faced. The Judean wilderness was a hot, rocky landscape, inhabited by wild animals. Why was it necessary for Jesus to begin his ministry in such a difficult way? Mark believed that this testing time was important preparation for Jesus' work. His experience of God's protection from wild beasts must have reassured him when he later faced opposition from powerful enemies. Similarly, surviving the inhospitable wilderness must have assured him of God's provision, when he later wandered from town to town, teaching, without a home of his own. Above all, his success in resisting the temptations of Satan confirmed his authority over evil and sin, something which would be central to his ministry.

Can you see God at work in any testing times you are going through? Are those challenges strengthening or weakening your faith? What difference does it make to know that Jesus was tested too?

Talk to God about any testing times you are going through and be honest about the struggles. Pray, too, for Christians you know who are going through hard times.

BIBLE IN A YEAR: **Isaiah 25,26; Psalm 104**

Who is Jesus?

Nothing can 'separate us from the love of God that is in Christ Jesus our Lord.'[1] Thank God for this wonderful truth.

One piece of advice commonly given to budding writers is 'show, don't tell': don't, for example, tell the reader that a character is confident. Instead show it in how they behave and appear. Mark could be said to be using the 'show, don't tell' principle in today's passage because, rather than stating that Jesus is God's Messiah, he shows it through the Lord's actions.

First, he describes Jesus astounding those in the synagogue with his teaching. Unlike the teachers of the law, who merely passed on the insights of rabbis before them, Jesus appears to have brought fresh revelation. We aren't told what Jesus taught them, because Mark wants the focus to be upon the authority with which he taught and where this came from. That Jesus believed he spoke with divine authority is reflected in how he introduces his teachings in the Sermon on the Mount with: 'You have heard that it was said to the people long ago ... But I tell you that ...'.[2]

Mark also demonstrates Jesus' authority over evil. This is reflected not simply in his ability to cast out an unclean spirit but in the ease with which he did it: a simple command and the spirit fled. That this was no mean feat is reflected in the disciples' failure to cast a demon out of a boy later in the Gospel.[3]

Mark expects us, like the witnesses of these events, to be astounded at Jesus' authority. He hoped his readers would realise that this showed Jesus to be God's chosen one, the Messiah. Are we astounded by Jesus – or has our image of him dwindled into little more than a nice man and a good teacher? Do we really believe he has complete power and authority over evil? What difference would believing that make in our lives?

Spend time reflecting on how Jesus astounded those who witnessed his works. With this powerful picture of Christ in mind, hand to him your fears and struggles.

[1] Rom 8:38,39   [2] Eg Matt 5:21,22   [3] Mark 9:14–29

BIBLE IN A YEAR: **Isaiah 27,28; Philemon 1**

The Right Priorities

Spend time giving over to God everything that is fighting for your attention: all the things you have to do and the worries you have.

After healing so many throughout the night, Jesus was exhausted and withdrew to pray. Simon Peter's reaction to this is interesting. We are told that he and the other disciples went to 'look for' Jesus (v 36), but the Greek conveys something a bit pushier: he tracked him down, almost hunted him.[1] Simon Peter was clearly frustrated with Jesus. After all, things were going great in Capernaum and there were still so many desperate people to heal. He may also have been stressed by the numbers of people crowding around his house seeking healing and may have wanted Jesus to return to take some of the pressure off.

All this led Peter to disturb Jesus' prayers and pressurise him to hurry back to Capernaum. Many of us would have caved in to such pressure but Jesus had a clear idea of God's plans. His prayers would have guided him, and his priority was doing God's will, even if others, including his friends, thought he was letting people down.

Jesus did not seek to tackle every problem and meet every need. He knew the importance of following God's direction and so left the crowds in Capernaum to go to teach elsewhere. Do we recognise the importance of discovering God's priorities for us, or does prayer get pushed out by the pressures and busyness of life? Do we take on roles and tasks to please others, or because we think God wants us to? How easy do we find it to say 'no' to misguided pressure? Let's recognise that if Christ had to say 'no' to many things that seemed like good ideas, so will we. Let's support our leaders in this, too, by not pressuring them to be overly busy and by praying that our churches are following God's priorities rather than doing too much.

Are you facing pressures to take on more than you should? Do you know what God wants you to prioritise and focus upon? Pray about these things.

[1] DE Nineham, *Saint Mark*, Penguin, 1963, p84

BIBLE IN A YEAR: **Isaiah 29,30; Hebrews 1**

Beyond Healing

'... as far as the east is from the west, so far has he removed our transgressions from us.'[1] Meditate on this verse and give thanks.

Today's reading continues Mark's focus on Jesus' identity. He has already shown Jesus' authority in teaching and over evil and now he shows it in his power to forgive.

This story can be difficult to interpret. By linking his ability to forgive sins with his healing of the paralysed man, Jesus appears to be suggesting that the man's disability was a result of his sin. However, his teaching elsewhere shows that he did not believe that those suffering from sickness, disability or misfortune are more sinful than anyone else. For example, John's Gospel records an incident where the disciples asked whether a man was blind because he or his family had done wrong: Jesus responds, 'Neither this man nor his parents sinned'.[2] The teachers of the law, however, did believe sickness resulted from sin, so Jesus was using their beliefs to box them into a corner. According to their doctrines, Jesus would only be able to heal the paralysed man by forgiving his sins. As they believed only God could forgive, Jesus was confronting them with his God-given authority by healing the man.

Unfortunately, simplistic beliefs such as those the teachers of the law had about sin and sickness are still around today. In one of her books, Joni Eareckson Tada, who was paralysed in her teens, describes a difficult encounter with a young Christian.[3] His understanding of the story in our passage led him to conclude that Joni remained unhealed because of unconfessed sin and a lack of faith. Fortunately, Joni was able to challenge him. God has worked through her in remarkable ways since her paralysis; her ministry has touched people worldwide, reminding us that God's power is not restricted to healing. It is also revealed mightily in the lives of those who continue to suffer and find strength in the Lord to keep going.

If this has raised difficult issues for you, share your thoughts with God and ask for a fresh sense of his love and acceptance.

---

[1] Ps 103:12 [2] John 9:3 [3] Joni Eareckson Tada, *A Place of Healing*, David C Cook, 2010, p15–17

BIBLE IN A YEAR: **Isaiah 31,32; Psalm 105**

The Special One

What different images of Jesus have you come across? What aspects of Christ do these images reflect?

This psalm is difficult. It is not always obvious who is speaking in it or who is being addressed, and its description of God as one who heaps up the dead (v 6) is uncomfortable.

For Jews of Jesus' day, however, the psalm was clear and its message a positive one. They took it to be about the Messiah. They believed he would be a descendant of King David, who would crush their enemies through military victory.[1] It is not surprising, then, that Jesus would quote from this psalm when debating with the Pharisees about the Messiah.[2] However, rather than using the psalm to confirm the Pharisees' beliefs, he used it to challenge their idea that the Messiah would be nothing more than a nationalistic military leader. He appears to have shared their belief that David wrote the psalm and that in verse 1 David is talking about the Messiah, calling him 'my Lord'. He argues that if the Messiah was simply a descendant of David, then David would not have called him 'my Lord'; there was more to the Messiah than that. As William Barclay says, Jesus was not just the son of David but the son of God too.[3]

Similarly, the reference in verse 4 to Melchizedek, the priestly king who blessed Abram in Genesis 14:18–20, is also used in the New Testament to heighten our understanding of Jesus' nature and work.[4] Melchizedek was seen as prefiguring Christ, being a priestly king who (because no reference is made to his birth or death) was believed to be a high priest for ever. The arguments follow a logic not easy for us to understand today. However, Jesus and the early church used this psalm to help us understand how unique and special Jesus is. How special is Jesus to you?

List everything you love about Jesus. Then consider if there is anything important about him you have omitted from your list.

---

[1] William Barclay, *The Gospel of Matthew*, Vol 2, Saint Andrew Press, 1988, p279 [2] Matt 22:41–46 [3] Barclay, 1988, p280 [4] Especially Heb 6:20 – 7:28

BIBLE IN A YEAR: **Isaiah 33,34; Hebrews 2**

Doing Things Differently

Have you ever felt like an outsider? What does it mean to know that God loves and accepts you?

Jesus angers religious leaders again in today's reading, this time by calling a tax collector to be his disciple and eating with him and his associates. Tax collectors were very unpopular with the general population, not just with the Pharisees, because they had a reputation for charging higher taxes than they should, to line their own pockets. It was shocking for Jesus to choose a disciple from such a line of work. Many would have questioned whether Jesus was a man of God after seeing him share meals with Levi and his associates, including his fellow tax collectors and others the religious authorities considered sinners. Sharing a meal was deeply symbolic to devout Jews: it was a sign of acceptance and close fellowship. No wonder the Pharisees struggled with Jesus' activities! Because they pursued religious purity, they avoided those they considered a bad influence. Jesus looked at things differently, though: he knew that sinners could not pull him away from God and believed he could bring them back to the Lord by mixing with them and showing them God's love.

The Pharisees get a bad press, but they were genuinely trying to obey God and make Israel a holy people, so avoiding those who were not serious about God made sense to them. Jesus' stated mission, however, was to seek and save the lost.[1] He realised that the Pharisees' focus and his desire to reach out were at loggerheads. His analogy of not sewing new, unshrunk cloth onto old or pouring young, still fermenting wine into old inflexible wineskins is about recognising when old traditions, no matter how well meant, restrict God's people and hold them back from doing God's work. Can we think of any traditions, structures, or ways of doing things that hinder us from continuing Jesus' work as effectively as we might?

Pray for the church, both locally and nationally, that it may be open to change when the Spirit prompts it.

---

[1] Luke 19:10

BIBLE IN A YEAR: **Isaiah 35,36; Hebrews 3**

Love Comes First

'Because of the LORD's great love we are not consumed, for his compassions never fail.'[1] Meditate on this verse.

The Pharisees continue to be antagonistic towards Jesus. Today we see them object to the disciples' plucking ears of grain and rubbing them between their fingers.[2] In their view this broke the commandment not to work on the Sabbath, for they counted this activity as reaping and threshing grain. Jesus countered their argument by reminding them that when David fled from Saul he broke religious law too, the law which forbade anyone other than a priest from eating the loaves of bread.[3] Scripture records this incident but does not criticise David for his actions, the implication being that appeasing his hunger and that of his men was more important than adhering to the rules.

Jesus argues that in a similar way people's needs take priority over the Sabbath regulations of the Pharisees: he argues that the Sabbath was created to benefit us, not weigh us down with laws that prevent us from helping others. Indeed, we read elsewhere of how frustrated Jesus got when the Pharisees condemned him for healing on the Sabbath.[4]

The principle Jesus presents has relevance for more than how we keep the Sabbath. Jesus prioritised the needs of people and refused to let rules, regulations and traditions get in the way of that. What would Jesus say, for instance, about objections to a food bank in church because it spoils the aesthetics; or opposition to a crèche because it creates noise in the service; or reluctance to create a disabled access because changes will need to be made to much-loved parts of a church building? Can you think of any ways this principle may apply to any decisions you are involved in? Let's pray that Jesus' love for those in need may be the dominating principle in our lives.

Pray for any situations known to you where there is conflict or disagreement over a way forward in church. Pray that God's love and his priorities will prevail.

---

[1] Lam 3:22 [2] Luke 6:1 [3] 1 Sam 21:1–6 [4] Mark 3:1–6; Luke 13:10–17; Matt 12:9–14; John 7:23

BIBLE IN A YEAR: **Isaiah 37,38; Hebrews 4**

Making a Stand

'O who am I, / that for my sake / my Lord should take / frail flesh and die?'[1]

The Pharisees taught that a person could only be healed on the Sabbath if she or he were dying. The man with the shrivelled hand did not fall into that category, so the Pharisees watched to see if Jesus would break their rules and heal him. Jesus knew they sought to trap him. He could have avoided trouble by healing him the next day or by doing it somewhere less public. However, he called the man into the middle of the synagogue, where everyone would see, and addressed the Pharisees' plot head on. His question silenced them, for they would either have to accept he was right to heal and go against their teaching or admit that their view on Sabbath-keeping prevented people from doing good on that holy day. By stopping good deeds from happening, the Pharisees could be seen to be aligning themselves with evil.[2]

His bold healing and public humiliation of the Pharisees enraged them so much that they joined forces with their enemies the Herodians to plot Jesus' death. As a religious group they did not have the power to execute him. They hoped the Herodians, political allies of Herod Antipas, ruler of Galilee, could persuade him to execute Jesus, just as he would later execute John the Baptist.

Jesus showed real bravery in healing the man and confronting the Pharisees. How did he have such courage? He was not exempt from the fear of death, as his agony in the Garden of Gethsemane shows.[3] Gethsemane also reveals, though, that wrestling in prayer gave him the strength to face the cross. No doubt his regular times of prayer throughout his ministry helped him deal with opposition. This encourages us that, if we lack the boldness to do what God wants, we can find it through prayer.

What do you need courage for? Pray for the strength and courage you need and for others known to you who need courage to do God's will.

---

[1] Samuel Crossman, 1623–83, 'My Song is Love Unknown' [2] CEB Cranfield, *The Gospel according to Saint Mark*, CUP, 1974, p120 [3] Luke 22:41–44

BIBLE IN A YEAR: Isaiah 39,40; Psalm 106

Mark 3:7–19

Simply the Best?

List ten things you can thank God for and praise him.

Despite the Pharisees' hostility to Jesus, his popularity with ordinary folk continued to grow and he was surrounded by a large number of people. Many of them had journeyed considerable distances to be healed. Others appear to have regularly travelled around with him.[1] It was from this group of followers that Jesus selected the twelve.

Despite having many people around him to choose from, those he called as apostles were not obvious choices. Simon Peter was impulsive and would go on to deny Jesus not long after promising him his undying loyalty. John and James were nicknamed 'sons of thunder' (v 17), possibly because they wanted to send down fire to burn a non-receptive village![2] Matthew is probably another name for the tax collector Levi, who was in a profession renowned for its corruption. Simon was nicknamed 'the Zealot' (v 18), suggesting that he may have been part of a political group wedded to violence. Thomas would famously go on to doubt Jesus' resurrection; and, of course, Judas would betray him.

Why did Jesus pick these men? The only clue Mark gives us is their full-blown commitment. Peter and Andrew left their fishing business 'at once' to follow Christ and similarly John and James appear to respond straightaway and leave their father and their nets behind.[3] Levi, too, forfeits his livelihood at the tax booth to follow Jesus without any apparent hesitation.[4] In today's passage we are simply told that Jesus 'called to him those he wanted, and they came to him' (v 13). When we select people for church roles, how important is a candidate's love for and commitment to Christ? How can we assess that? What encouragement can we take personally from Jesus' choice of the twelve?

Pray for anyone who struggles to believe God can work through them, that their confidence in Christ may increase.

---

[1] Eg Jesus' appointment of 72 for his mission, Luke 10:1 [2] Luke 9:54 [3] See Mark 1:18–20 [4] Mark 2:14

BIBLE IN A YEAR: **Isaiah 41,42; Hebrews 5**

Dangerous Lies

'Come near to God and he will come near to you.'[1] Quieten your heart before the Lord.

Jesus now faces further opposition, this time from an unexpected quarter. His family arrive to seize him and take him home, believing him to be 'out of his mind' (v 21). Perhaps the criticism he'd received from religious leaders and his association with society's outcasts alarmed them.[2] They may have worried about his lifestyle, as crowds constantly pressed in on him, placing him in physical danger and making it difficult for him to have time to eat (v 20). Whatever the reason, it must have been painful for Jesus to be misunderstood by his own family.

The opposition of the religious authorities was different: they were not confused about Jesus. They could see that his mighty works could only be the result of God's power, yet they denied this to discredit him. They even claimed he could cast out demons because he was himself possessed by the prince of demons (v 22).

Jesus' warning about an unforgivable sin often worries people. The religious leaders were in danger of this, because they knowingly lied about Jesus. Their hearts were so set against him that they declared this godly man, evil. Their hardened consciences would prevent them from repenting and so deny them forgiveness.[3] Few will ever be guilty of this extreme sin. Instead, our focus should be on Jesus' comforting words that 'people can be forgiven all' other 'sins and every slander' (v 28). This forgiveness is illustrated by the changed attitude of Jesus' family in later years. Despite their initial doubts, his mother and some, at least, of his brothers went on to become his followers.[4] Indeed, his brother James was so committed that he led the church in Jerusalem and was martyred for his faith – stoned to death, according to Josephus.[5]

Pray for anyone who finds it hard to believe God can forgive them or who is struggling to repent. Pray that their eyes may be opened to God's amazing grace.

---

[1] James 4:8 [2] William Barclay, *The Gospel of Mark*, Westminster John Knox Press, 2017, p71 [3] Barclay, p77 [4] Acts 1:12–14 [5] *Antiquities of the Jews*, 20, 199–203

BIBLE IN A YEAR: **Isaiah 43,44; Hebrews 6**

Mark 4:1–20

No Turning Back?

What prayers of yours has God answered recently? Give thanks.

My son often asks, 'Why doesn't God make himself known to the world so obviously that no one could ever doubt his existence?' Today's reading would frustrate my son further, because it seems that rather than making it easy for people to believe, Jesus deliberately obscures his message by speaking in parables. In addition, the parable of the sower makes it clear that most people (three out of four of the groups who hear the gospel) either fail to keep going in their faith or never believe in the first place.

Clearly, Jesus thought there was benefit in making his listeners work at understanding his message. It has been said that the parables are ways of sifting out those who are genuinely interested in becoming disciples from those who are not.[1] Jesus seems to want people to make a choice to follow him, and his story of the sower shows why: following Christ is not easy. It is important to go into faith with our eyes open: there is a cost involved and, just as the growth of the seeds on rocky ground failed when the sun beat down, many will not keep going when following Christ gets tough. Do we make the cost of discipleship clear when we present the Christian message, or are we so keen to win people over that we water down our words into ones of comfort without cost?

The pressures of life and materialism are other stumbling blocks. How easy it is for God to get pushed out by 'the worries of this life, the deceitfulness of wealth and the desires for other things' (v 19). In what ways do these interfere with our growth as Christians? How comforting do you find the parable's ending that, if we persist, we will experience great fruitfulness?

Dear Lord, please help me to keep growing in faith and fruitfulness. I'm sorry for when I allow things to distract me from my devotion to you.

[1] R Alan Cole, *Mark*, IVP, 1988, p88

BIBLE IN A YEAR: **Isaiah 45,46; Psalm 107**

Look Back in Thankfulness

'I thank my God every time I remember you.'[1] Who can you thank God for?

The focus of this psalm is on the great deeds of God and the importance of studying them. Commentators believe that the deeds the psalmist primarily had in mind were to do with the beginnings of Israel and events such as God's deliverance of his people from Egypt.[2]

Why is it important to take time to thank God, not only for his deeds recorded in Scripture but also for all he has done for us on a personal level? First, it's easy to move on too quickly from answered prayer to focus on the next problem that faces us. I know I sometimes forget I have prayed about something and fail to appreciate how God has been at work answering my prayers. Taking time to recognise and give thanks for answered prayer builds up our faith, for it reminds us of God's goodness. This is also important to do because life isn't one miraculous event after the other.

The Jews who experienced the Exodus would wander forty years in the desert before entering the Promised Land. During this time, they grumbled against God and forgot his goodness to them. Even once they'd possessed Canaan, they would continue to face problems, most notably the Babylonian invasion and their Exile in that foreign land. The Jews needed to keep remembering God's past deeds to be able to trust him in the hard times.

Where are you? Have you just witnessed God do amazing things? Ensure that you take time to fully appreciate that. Give thanks and dwell on what this teaches you about God's nature. Or are you in the wilderness, wondering if God has forgotten you? Build up your faith by remembering and giving thanks for the things God has done for you in the past, for he is faithful still.

Take two minutes to list as many answers to prayer as you can think of. Give thanks for them and reflect on what they teach you of God's nature.

---

[1] Phil 1:3 [2] John Goldingay, *Psalms Vol 3*, Baker Academic, 2008, p30

BIBLE IN A YEAR: **Isaiah 47,48; Hebrews 7**

Mark 4:21–25

Putting in the Work

Read again a favourite passage of Scripture and thank God for the truths it contains.

Some of Jesus' sayings in this passage are particularly difficult to understand. What, for instance, is the meaning of 'Those who have will be given more; as for those who do not have, even what they have will be taken from them' (v 25, TNIV)? Is this justification for the adage that the rich get richer and the poor get poorer? On a similar front, sociologist Robert K Merton was inspired by Matthew's version of this verse[1] to coin the phrase 'the Matthew effect'. This describes the tendency for established scientists to get the credit for discoveries younger scientists have also made, simply because they are better known.[2]

Jesus, however, is not saying that he supports the 'haves' over the 'have-nots'. His words are a continuation of his teaching on parables begun in the parable of the sower. He is exhorting people to put effort into growing in their understanding of his teaching by stating the principle true of all learning – that the more effort we put in, the more we will understand. His warning that those 'who do not have' will lose even what they do have, rings true for anyone who has tried to learn a language. Neglect practising your new language skills for too long and you quickly forget what you once knew. This is true of our spiritual growth too. We need to keep putting effort in to understanding and applying God's Word, so we don't go backwards but keep on growing.

How can we do that? We can dig deeper. When we do not understand a passage, or if an explanation of a Bible reading doesn't answer our questions, we can try and find out more for ourselves: read commentaries, search the internet, ask others. It's easy to settle for what we already know, but standing still isn't really an option in God's kingdom.

What do you think you can do to ensure that you continue to grow in your understanding and application of God's Word?

[1] Matt 13:12 [2] http://www.garfield.library.upenn.edu/merton/matthew1.pdf

BIBLE IN A YEAR: **Isaiah 49,50; Hebrews 8**

Unstoppable

Give thanks for growth you have seen in yourself and in others.

Mark's Gospel is often said to have a particular focus upon suffering and it is thought that this may be because his first readers faced persecution.[1] Although we may not suffer in the same way these early Christians did, none of us lead a trouble-free life in this fallen world. We can all point to times when Jesus did great things in our lives but also to other times when troubles loomed and God seemed distant. God's kingdom has broken into our lives through Jesus but, until he returns, the world is still plagued by evil. Mark reflects this tension between 'the now and the not yet' of the kingdom in Jesus' life too: he believes that Jesus' healings, exorcisms and teaching make it clear who Jesus really is. However, he also shows us that many, including religious leaders and members of Jesus' own family, rejected his ministry. Mark also describes Jesus' caution in revealing his identity: teaching those outside his inner circle

only in parables, silencing evil spirits when they declared him to be God's chosen one and asking people not to tell others of their healing.[2] Although he came to reveal God's kingdom, he had to do this carefully, in a world where many would oppose and misunderstand him.

The parables in today's reading must have encouraged Mark's original audience in their suffering and can encourage us too. It's easy to despair when we see church numbers dwindling and when we find it tough being Christians in an unsympathetic world. These parables encourage us that, no matter how unpromising things may appear, nothing can stop the miraculous growth of the kingdom. The mustard seed, despite its tiny beginnings, could grow up to become a tall tree. So, let's not lose hope, for nothing can stop the progress of God's kingdom.

Share with God any ways in which you feel disheartened and thank him that he is at work even when we struggle to see it.

[1] John Drane, *Introducing the New Testament*, Lion Publishing, 1999, p198 [2] Mark 1:25,34,43,44; 3:11,12; 5:43; 7:33–36

BIBLE IN A YEAR: **Isaiah 51,52; Hebrews 9**

Mark 4:35–41

Don't Panic!

'God is our refuge and strength, an ever-present help in trouble. Therefore we will not fear, though the earth give way and the mountains fall'.[1]

The artist Rembrandt's painting 'The Storm on the Sea of Galilee' portrays the events of this passage dramatically. In his picture a huge wave pushes the fishing boat up into a forty-five-degree angle as the disciples desperately cling on to ropes and sails for their very lives. It brings out the real danger the disciples were in – and for these fishermen to panic things must have been really bad! Many of them had worked on this lake all their lives. They were used to handling difficult weather conditions for, although the Sea of Galilee is really a lake, it was renowned for sudden and severe storms. High waves were swamping the disciples' boat and the lives of those on board were in real jeopardy.

Jesus, however, is sound asleep at the back of the boat, exhausted after teaching huge crowds. He appears completely unaware of the danger they are in. No wonder the disciples accuse him of not caring. They are only crossing the lake because he has told them to and yet he is asleep rather than helping when his instructions lead them into trouble.

Most of us will have felt like the disciples at some time for, as the story shows, doing what Jesus asks of us does not mean we will avoid trouble – and it may even lead us into it. Many of us have questioned why Christ feels absent just when we need him most and wondered in difficult times if he has forgotten us. This story encourages us to have faith, though, for we do not need to fear. Even when it doesn't feel like it, Jesus is with us amid the storm and he really does care. The one who silenced the wind and the waves will see us safely through our troubles too.

Are you going through any storms at the moment? How well are you doing, trusting God throughout this time? Be honest about your feelings and ask for his help.

---

[1] Ps 46:1,2

BIBLE IN A YEAR: **Isaiah 53,54; Psalms 108,109**

THERE IS NO OTHER GOD

2 Kings starts with Ahaziah the king of Israel intending to consult foreign gods when he was injured. Elijah asks him, 'is it because there is no God in Israel ...?' (1:6,16). This chapter and the subsequent ones repeatedly demonstrate, through an abundance of miraculous stories, that there is, indeed, a God in Israel. God primarily works through 'the man of God' (1:9,10,11,12,13), Elijah, until Elisha takes over his mantle in chapter 2. Whereas Israel's king behaves as if there is no God in Israel, two foreigners do turn to God in their sickness, notably the Aramaean army commander Naaman in chapter 5 and Ben-Hadad the king of Aram in chapter 8. Naaman even declares, 'Now I know that there is no God in all the world except in Israel' (5:15). The Israelite woman from Shunem, too, is a faithful believer in God (4;8–10; 8:1–6). She is a recurring character and demonstrates that God is interested in everyday matters and affairs.

Elisha is concerned with the northern kingdom of Israel, as opposed to the southern kingdom of Judah – the twelve tribes split into two kingdoms after Solomon dies. Samaria is a key city in the northern kingdom and throughout this time is involved in wars and skirmishes with other nations. When the book starts, Moab is a key enemy, but by the end of chapter 8, Aram has besieged Samaria and continues to be an ominous threat. It is ironic that Aram's king and the commander of its army should enquire of their enemy's prophet and God in times of sickness.

Not long after asking for a double portion of Elijah's spirit, Elisha used that power to curse young boys (2:9,23,24). The story is open to different understandings. Does God then vindicate Elisha? Or, given the Bible's emphasis on compassion and mercy elsewhere, does Elisha misuse divine power? The incident is not too dissimilar to Elijah's calling down fire from heaven (ch 1), but where Elijah's life was at risk, Elisha was merely mocked.

Julie Woods

The Lion Roars

Lord, who shut the mouths of lions for Daniel, you sometimes roar yourself. May I harken to the roar in this passage and remember that 'The LORD – he is God!'[1]

As an Israelite king, Ahaziah should have led the people in the way of the Lord. Instead, Ahaziah's first inclination is to pray to a foreign god. Does he think that his own God does not know whether he will recover? His messengers do not get as far as enquiring of this false god, however, because God sends Elijah to intercept them.

Three times we hear the question, 'Is it because there is no God in Israel …?' (vs 3,6,16). The first time is when the angel tells Elijah what he is to say, the second when the king's messengers tell Ahaziah what Elijah said to them, and on the third occasion the words come directly from Elijah to the king. By that point, God has made it quite clear that there is a God in Israel. The consuming fire verifies Elijah as a man of God –

Elijah had prayed, 'If I am a man of God, may fire come down' (v 10).

This event is reminiscent of 1 Kings 18 where, in the days of King Ahab, Elijah had been in conflict with the prophets of Baal. The fire of the Lord had come down and consumed the sacrifice and the sacrificial area as well as the water. On that occasion, the people fell on their faces and repeated, 'The LORD – he is God'.[1] Had Ahab's son, Ahaziah, forgotten that occurrence? Elijah could never have defended himself against an army of fifty, but with God's protection and intervention he was saved. The roar of the Lion clearly shows not only that there is a God in Israel, but that he protects his messengers. We also know, as Elijah surely did, that Elijah's demonstrations only show a fraction of God's power – a lion's power does not lie in its roar.

'… is it because there is no God for you to consult …?' (v 16). God gives brains, friends, the internet, etc for decision-making, but do you turn to God's Word first?

[1] 1 Kings 18:39

BIBLE IN A YEAR: **Isaiah 55,56; Hebrews 10**

Gifts and Responsibility

Dear God, please help me to develop the gifts you have given me and to use them wisely, discerningly, responsibly and sensitively.

There are puzzling aspects in this well-known passage, where the mantle of Elijah literally passes to Elisha. Why does Elisha tell the company of the prophets to be quiet? Why does the company of prophets look for Elijah (vs 16,17) when they know he is being taken from Elisha that day? There are issues with the two bears mauling the 42 boys.

God had given foreknowledge to the prophets. Perhaps they felt the need to inform Elisha of Elijah's imminent departure. Maybe they wanted to test whether he already knew, as an indicator of how worthy a successor he would be. Either way, it seems insensitive. Elisha is about to lose someone close to him (tearing his cloak later probably indicates mourning) and it would be natural for him to require quiet. Until Elijah is taken from him, Elisha does not initiate conversation – he simply answers questions and insists on sticking close to his master. Despite their foreknowledge and witnessing of the seamless transition of prophetic role from the hairy Elijah to the bald Elisha with the Moses-like parting of the waters, the prophets want to search for Elijah. They appear not to have pondered the significance of their God-given knowledge nor how best to use it.

Having demonstrated that he has received the requested 'double portion' of God's spirit (vs 9–12,15), Elisha brings life by purifying waters. When God gives gifts, however, he does not take away free will and one can misuse God-given gifts. Elisha's anger, and perhaps fear, flares when he is mocked, and he responds with a destructive curse. His actions are open to various understandings, as is the verb sometimes translated 'maul'. It means 'cleave, break open, through, into' and since two bears are unlikely to maul 42 boys, might best be translated 'break into/scatter.'

Employ well the gifts God has given you. Repent for times you have wielded them as weapons, been lazy in developing them, or insensitive in using them.

BIBLE IN A YEAR: **Isaiah 57,58; Hebrews 11**

2 Kings 3

Facing Against Face Value

Lord God, there are many parts of Scripture that I do not understand and some parts, even, that I may not like. Help me to learn in submission to you.

In this chapter, Elisha is instrumental in bringing about another miracle concerning water. He also executes a different kind of miraculous event, for the Moabites mistake the water for blood when they see the sun shining on it. These two events lead to Israel winning the battle.

The ending is troubling. The Moabites make a human sacrifice and then a great fury comes on Israel and they withdraw. It might be that the battle goes against Israel (perhaps the Moabites were inspired by the public sacrifice), but commentators have also suggested (eg Hobbs in the *Word* commentary series) that the Israelites withdraw in disgusted fury. The wider context of the Old Testament precludes the possibility that a human sacrifice to a foreign god would have been effective.

In chapter 1, King Ahaziah fell through the lattice window and injured himself, so he wanted to enquire of foreign gods if he would recover. On the face of it, it might have seemed to Ahaziah that the God of Israel was ineffectual, for he did not prevent the king's fall. As readers of faith, we can easily fall into the trap of thinking that we would have behaved better and would not have been tempted to doubt God or his power. On the face of it, the ending to chapter 3 suggests the human sacrifice works, for the Israelites go home. Perhaps we are now in a quandary. Do the foreign gods after all have power to accept a human sacrifice and to turn the tide of war against God's people? Such thinking brings us closer to Ahaziah, for we too are now doubting God's power by looking no further than the face of the situation, even though we have just read a few verses earlier of God's miraculous interventions.

Interpreting Scripture well is both an art and a science, needing practice and discernment. We may frequently get it wrong, but let our starting point be God's goodness and power.